To Suffer Is

Divine

The Revival Of A

Soul

A Book Of Poetry

By

Angella Brevitz

ISBN: 978-1-937089-73-3

Truth Book Publishers
www.truthbookpublisher.com

First Printing 2020

Table of Content

Dedication

To my babies, my blessings from God to help me lead us right back to Him. May He guide you on his path of love and righteousness. I love you more than words could ever express my beautiful children.

Foreword

In this book of poems, the author is telling a story using poetry to reveal the story of her life. Angella's book of poems is a companion to her book, "From Murder To Grace."

The poetry compliments her life long story of finding purpose for her life. As she wonderfully tells her story through poems the reader will be intrigued as she weaves in and out of her webs of trouble. Thus, leading the reader through the thoughts of her soul.

She openly speaks to pain and hurt that one goes through as they try to gain insight on the many struggles of life. Her poems points to something that comes deep down within her heart and mind on issues she has encountered through no fault of her own. Yet, through the canvas of poetry she pens some of the most hurtful moments of her life. Giving you the reader an inside look on how God will ultimately tie everything together.

Angella's prose enables her to weave her way into the real issue we all must face, that is, rediscovering God through Christ. She like many others discovered through her many failures that true love only comes as God's Holy Spirit takes us to Christ. Each of her poems systematically enlightens those that have experienced deep hurt and pain. Through her poetry she speaks about abstract things such as Fear, Forgiveness and Despair.

Her book of poems is a must read because it subtly answers the questions that one goes through as they find the answers to "Why." Her poems read like a cat and mouse chase to victory over the real enemy. More than anything it is a provocative look of her life as she learns to adapt to the many trials and tribulations. Each of her poems will give you the reader a clear understanding of "Why." Angella's hope is that her poetry pulls those hurting into a relationship with Christ.

Bishop Joe M. Fears

Introduction

This compilation of poetry is only possible because of what Christ Jesus did in leaving us His Holy Spirit. All the glory goes to God in giving me the words and the strength to endure. I began writing at the age of 14. Thereafter, I would write when I was in pain, confused, or just needed to release my feelings. I had no way of knowing that 25 years later God would allow me to put them all together and share them with the world. I see now how he chooses people to go through painful things for His purposes and His glory. If we are able to keep going despite the obstacles He will always give us clarity and make a way through.

I chose to write a book about my life after many years of knowing I would. I had included my poetry in my autobiography. When I had my book all ready for editing my brother in Christ told me to separate the poetry because I had an entire book in those alone. I believe that is how God wants it to be. There is power in suffering; although it never feels very good. My poetry reveals the heart of suffering in this world and also a longing for something more. My poems show clearly that we all long for God whether we know it or not. My life was heartache after heartache searching for something or someone to fill a void that was created by God and only He can fill. Through the transitions, seasons, and pain, my outlook began to shift. I am anchored in the Lord at this point. There is a clear and distinctive difference in my writing after I began to give my life to Jesus.

This book is one of my greatest life's work and I am so grateful that I never gave up as I was suicidal and hopeless before finding The Lord. My only hope in publishing this book is that someone will find hope and strength in their suffering knowing that God has a plan for all of our life struggles. There is never such a thing as too far gone, no matter who you are or what you have done. God can and will forgive you, heal you, give you His Holy Spirit, and prepare you for His will. My prayer is that these poems give living proof of this because I am alive today.

Angella Brevitz

I forgive You

I forgive you for not knowing. I forgive you for trying. I forgive you for hurting me. I forgive you for being so hard on yourself. I forgive you for having a baby at 16. I forgive you for making bad decisions. I forgive you for being in that truck that night. I forgive you for not telling. I forgive you for not loving me. I forgive you, so just let it be!

°•o⊙o•° ... °•o⊙o•° ... °•o⊙o•°

One Step

Despite me and all my flaws he loves me still no matter what. It took some time to truly see just how much our Father loves me. Through all the searching, heartache, and tears he has been here throughout the years!

There was a time I could not see Sweet Jesus is right here with me. I walked through life lost and confused, I wanted love yet received abuse. The one constant thing through it all is that Jesus picks me up every time I fall!

I would often wonder how I survived all the trials and tribulations throughout my life. See even if we choose not to believe God stays with us, he never leaves. He loves us more than we love ourselves, he never puts us on a shelf.

He does not leave us forsakes us not, all we search for is found in God! So, look no more I tell you this, there is so much I don't want you to miss! Walk with him for a little while and soon you will know you are his child. When you know your Father has your back, yours is the victory no matter the attack!

It does not make life perfect or free from stress, but it puts your life in order, so you can be your best. He only loves you he does not hold a grudge, nothing you could do would change his love!

He is here to stay, and he wants to help, you Cannot do this life by yourself! So, take a step, just one will do, begin the process and watch   Abba move! Don't take my word, find out for yourself, Jesus is our only help!

°•o⊙o•°   ...   °•o⊙o•°   ...   °•o⊙o•°

Forgiveness

I must start by saying thank you, Yes, I am so deep down thankful! Not because I have material things, not because I have fulfilled my dreams. All because Jesus rescued me, I feel the rest is history!

I rest in a peace I have never known! I rest in this love on the cross freely shown! I am yours Jesus and you are mine! I don't have money, I don't need a dime! I gave it all up just listening to God, I know it sounds crazy, yet my feet are shod!

You humbled me Daddy and I thank you, for now, I can do what you need me to do. This world is lost, they are deceived, They don't even see they are perishing! Oh, but the hope of John 3:16, Your only begotten son you gave so free!

Jesus, when I think about your pain, my worries fade, it all goes away! You are so much stronger than me, they beat and crucified you physically! All you did was teach in truth and love, they mocked you, truly because they were jealous!

You didn't have money or wealth, Yet, you brought the sick back to health! There was power and authority in your words, you spoke the truth people had never heard! Now, many loved you and followed you, but those who were selfish hated you!

Either way you prayed the same, you took love out of all the hate! How truly powerful love is, especially when you are most hated! See, the law no man could fulfill, Yet the Pharisees preached as if they did!

When you came Jesus, you put them in their place, But so beautifully in love and grace! They could not contain the truth in you, So, they plotted to kill you and it came true. Truth is, it was Father God's plan to begin with, For the devil plots but Father God always wins!

You knew all along how it would end, you did it for us sinners, not for yourself! You ended it all with the most loving truth, Father forgive them for they know not what they do!

°•o(ı)o•°   ...   °•o(ı)o•°   ...   °•o(ı)o•°

The Ride

I call upon you, do you hear? Are you here God? Are you near? I really need to talk to you, so you can show me what to do. My life, it seems, didn't go as planned; not how I pictured the plane to land.

I thought it would be smooth and bump free, I forgot you already had plans for me. So, as I landed and almost crashed, I was reminded my plans won't last. I must know in my heart you and I can never be apart.

Not for one second, minute, or hour, Otherwise the enemy will steal, kill, and devour! See happiness comes from faith and trusting God above. Knowing he can do anything and gives us unconditional love.

When you know this you cannot be defeated, you cannot be lost, and you cannot be cheated. Everything simply comes together, any storm you now can weather. So, I beg of you please give in. God's plan for your life is a guaranteed win!

°•○◖◗○•° ... °•○◖◗○•° ... °•○◖◗○•°

Before Me

Old tattered heart with confused intentions. Somebody should have staged an intervention. Before me there was chaos, drama, and tears. Plenty of heartache and a lot of fears. Sunshine, but more rain, o before me!

You couldn't get through life very well. You paved a road right straight to hell. You didn't know, you tried your best. But that's the thing, with me, you rest. Your burdens are mine, just give them to me. I promise this is real; you're about to be set free.

See, I've been here all along waiting on you. I don't ever give up, it's just not what I do. So, I waited and watched, nurtured and pruned, Until you were completely transformed and constantly renewed. More and more you ask for me, so more and more I come to thee.

If it's me you seek, it is me you will find. Now that you know, why would you rewind time? Remember before me all the agony and pain? I Truly hope you don't go through that again! But if you choose, and you do, I will be right by your side to see you through. All because I love you endlessly. O what a wretched man before me!

°•○◉○•°   ...   °•○◉○•°   ...   °•○◉○•°

Beautifully Broken

I see a little girl as bright as a bulb; All the worldly problems if only she could solve!

Twirling... yes dancing lovingly around, Love flows freely in her heart it abounds! Yet she is always looking about, wishing love would make a loud shout. Quietly she sits in peace, Wondering... Do they notice me? Who am I? Do they even care? Would they miss me if I was no longer there? What a joy such as this little one, yet from her love seems to run!

But wait! Do you hear that? The living God, he is near that! He tells me he will give me my heart back! He reassures me my back he has always had! This world is terribly lost in evil sauce! They turn over every stone and at all costs! The babes are tortured yet already lost! Truly Father's babies need Jesus Christ the boss! Yet sadly, they mock him, they mock me. I see now it is just my destiny! Yes, no doubt it cuts sharp as a razor, it burns like fire, shocks like a Taser!

Then I remember all King Jesus did! He knew from youth, just a small kid! He didn't do as others around, He came for love and truth to be found! He already knew humans would disagree, yet still came from Heaven to save them, you, and me! He came to hell and knowing its cost, but to flesh he died and it was no loss! He wanted Father's babies who are lost. He humbly said, "Father I will pay their cost!" John 3:16 how perfect of a love, to send our Lord and Savior from above!

So many times, I lost my mind, yet every time, it is me I'd find! I'd pray and ask God to give me strength, and he sure did, love in a wink! Love in the stretching out of two arms. Love knowing its final hour of harm! Yet still, two arms Jesus stretched out wide; His blood on the dirt, no longer inside! From his enemies he would not hide, He didn't look left nor, did he look right! He only thought of crimson to white, So, he continued to love, to fight the good fight!

In that moment he tried to enjoy the ride, for truly he came the enemy to snide! The great liar always has plans and plots, yet he is dead. Destruction. Rot! He has hurt each soul, and often deep, To the point real love cannot be seen.

People complaining saying others are mean, well truly the battle we fight is an Ephesians thing! So, cry... it's okay to let go of hurt, it always shows you your true worth! It always comes with a rebirth, So, go ahead, just let it hurt!

Jesus knows all you truly deserve. He needs you to see what it really was that hurt. It was the evil one separating you, So, he could tell you what to do! But Father God always had a plan for you, so deep down you smiled and made it through! Now it's time to say goodbye, goodbye to the broken girl who cries!

For really those are not her tears, all those tears shed all those years! It is like headlights upon a deer, no longer a person does she fear! Because truly God heard her cries, from a pure heart in a world full of lies!

°•○ⓘo•°   ...   °•○ⓘo•°   ...   °•○ⓘo•°

Rebirth

For every heart that's broken, every life that's torn apart; there's a soul that is rebirthed and given a new start. This is not courageous, strong, or wise; this is the difference of close loving ties. When someone loves you just for you, Then You see clearly what you are capable to do. Not what others expect from you, rather what Makes you feel brand new.

When again the world turns grey, you just remember that special way. When someone close told you the truth. You are loved down to the you; The you no one else chose to love. The person you hated just because. Love is powerful, and love is strong. True unconditional love is never wrong.

When you are loved in these wonderful ways, your broken heart is completely amazed. Then you have been born again, when you realize you can count on them; Will they know what they have done? By just showing you unconditional love! Your life transformed right before your eyes; All because of close loving ties!

°•o(ᴊ)o•°   ...   °•o(ᴊ)o•°   ...   °•o(ᴊ)o•°

Torn

Through this all my emotions speak free, I feel All kinds talking to me. One says I should feel one way while another tries to lead me astray. I don't know on which to depend, I feel my world is coming to an end. Love and hate draw such a fine line, in my mind they both combine.

For there is you whom I hold so dear, yet you do much to be feared. The one who simply loves me, I tell myself I don't want to see. There were few I chose to love, I thought we fit just like a glove. You are gone with only memories to remain, what we've been through links us like a chain.

Is fate pulling you away from my heart, or were you simply never there from the start? The happiness I felt next to your touch, I miss that love so very much. Did I imagine you loved me so deep? Was I only a place to fall asleep? All these thoughts run through my head as I lay alone in a cold hard bed.

For loving you a high price I will pay, your actions leave me here to stay. I hope God will forgive your sins, and maybe you will find love from within.

°•o◌o•° ... °•o◌o•° ... °•o◌o•°

No Love

Why does it seem to be me, I'm always the one who's lonely? I just want someone I can trust, Not someone just looking for lust. Every time I meet someone new, it always seems too good to be true.

I think a lot about all the fun, the fun I'd Have with the right one. But, no one seems to come around, it's like I'm lost never to be found. They say somewhere there's a special soul, on to which your love will unfold.

How am I supposed to know who's true? When I Feel they are I end up blue? What's wrong with me, am I that bad? I hurt so much and feel so sad. Everyone seems to turn me down, The only thing I do is frown.

I can't remember being happy, or having fun and truly laughing. I guess I have to wait so long, but you know all those guys are wrong. Because underneath all this pain, I'm something, not a loss, a gain.

°•o◌o•° ... °•o◌o•° ... °•o◌o•°

My Baby Girl

You are my world, the reason I live. To you my life I would give. I struggle daily to take care of you. I know it's hard on you too. I give you everything that I have. You give enough just when you laugh. You bring me all the joy in the world.

You are my baby girl. I will always love you more, Than anything in this life before. You'll always be my number one. We always have so much fun. So, if you ever think different, just read   this and believe it. I love you baby girl!

°•o◯o•°   ...   °•o◯o•°   ...   °•o◯o•°

Rainbow

All alone I'm sitting here, this hard life is what I fear. I have plans and a dream, Things aren't always what they seem.

The hard road is what I've chose, some problems have made their pose. Yet, I keep going steady and strong, how long can I hold on?

All the tasks on my mind, I want to leave them all behind. I know I must have faith; my dreams will come to me someday. Someday the hard work will show, Like a pot of gold at the end of a rainbow.

°•o◯o•°   ...   °•o◯o•°   ...   °•o◯o•°

Anything

In a sea of green, you can do anything, just ask me any day of the week. I go and come and come and go but do I even really know?

The love we carry everywhere we go, sometimes we don't even know! Just how much that love can mean; just how much that love can gleam!

If we don't know just what we have then how can we be joyful and glad? So full of love, joy, and peace; this is what his love can bring.

But you must know just how much God loves you and also, just what he wants you to do. And how to love, and when, and who...

°•○◍○•° ... °•○◍○•° ... °•○◍○•°

Take and Give

I met up with you one day. We talked and laughed, you actually stayed. My happiness is what you give, All the love I need to live.

I feel as though my life's complete. My heart will break when you leave. This love's too good to be true, Especially from someone like you.

Everyone says how quick you'll cheat, when there's someone else you meet. I feel you love only me, And I too make your life complete.

But, if someday you shall go, I refuse to let you know. Inside my heart will break, A part of me you will take.

°•○◌○•° ... °•○◌○•° ... °•○◌○•°

Frenemies

I sit sometimes, I wonder why? Why do people want to see me die? Or do bad, or fall off, or be sad or completely lost. They continue to stab at my heart, And why? When they get what they want or need, they leave and don't say goodbye. Is it fair or is it nice? Who needs enemies with friends like this?

°•○◌○•° ... °•○◌○•° ... °•○◌○•°

Despair

I just can't handle this anymore, All I am is a little whore. No one loves me like they should, they say they do, I wish they would. I carry on day by day so depressed, it seems like I am always upset.

No one is here for me, I am all alone, I know you see. Sometimes I need a friend, every friendship is at its end. Just when I've got some support, it goes away so sweet and short.

My family doesn't love me the same, they all say that I am to blame. They don't know what I've become, they say I will be a bum. Someday I will show them all, then they might be the ones to fall.

°•○◌○•° ... °•○◌○•° ... °•○◌○•°

Murder

Why is it that I am to blame? People look at me with such a shame! Time goes by, still nothing changed. Here I sit, why do I remain?

To stick it out, to feel forgiven, enough pain and sorrow I have lived! People don't even know the real truth!

Sometimes I feel O so abused! My life was changed that night forever! I really wanted so much better! For them- for me- I never knew, What on God's green Earth did they do!?! It was not me; this I promise. God knows the truth, it's all around us!

If only I could live my life, With no judgement, with no strife! I hope, I pray, for better days! It seems this will never go away!

I made a mistake, I chose the wrong friends, will this nightmare ever end? Don't people realize God wants us to forgive?

If we don't, we never really live! I understand it can be hard, but dang I want to let down my guard! As I sit and write these truths, I realize I was just a youth!

°•ₒ◍ₒ•° ... °•ₒ◍ₒ•° ... °•ₒ◍ₒ•°

Choices

Love, what is it? Do we know? What does it take to make love grow? What is important in our lives? These decisions must be made wisely!

What we choose cannot be undone. Sometimes we choose the wrong one. The wrong choice, decision, or path, But, everyone has a chance to come back!

We learn from the things that we choose, almost always we must lose. No matter which way we go, which road we travel, we will have regrets everybody has them.

What will make us happy, we wonder? So many choices we have to ponder. We never really know what to do, we just choose what we choose.

We want what's best in our lives, sometimes we are our own demise!

°•○Ⓙ○•° ... °•○Ⓙ○•° ... °•○Ⓙ○•°

You and I

You told me how you cared for me, you expressed what you wanted us to be. I didn't believe all that you said, I felt that I was being misled. You told me that my friends were wrong, you said I'd understand, it wouldn't take long.

I told you what you said couldn't be true, I thought you just wanted my time for you. You said I was the one you searched for, you said you'd never leave my heart torn. I pushed you away because I didn't believe, I thought if I did you'd be the one to leave.

You tried to show me a better way to live, you taught me it's okay to take but it feels good to give. I tried, for a minute, to live how you taught, I didn't last long and turned my back with no thought. You were still there to show me the way, you saw you were losing and didn't know what to say.

I was distant and rude with you, I was doing so wrong and thought you never knew. I knew what I was doing and didn't know why, I didn't see then but it was all a big lie. I now sit here lonely with a clear mind, I can only think because all I have is time.

You told me all my friends weren't real, I never knew all they could steal. I called you very sad and scared, I don't know how I even dared. You said that you were still here for me, I know it took time for me to see, I now see what I want you and I to be, I can't show you because I'm no longer free.

°•o(ı)o•°   ...   °•o(ı)o•°   ...   °•o(ı)o•°

Seven

For those of you who never knew the little girl they found in you. The power given is unreal, but you don't know the way it feels. To look within and see yourself; the faults, the qualities, the knowledge of wealth.

Take a look at the child; the little girl they found inside. She is beautiful and full of life, you would never know she had a rough life. She seems to have completely forgotten; the terrible, awful, and the rotten.

To her dismay she feels blessed to this very day. For she has seen the other side. She says it is a scary ride. Yet on that ride she learned to see the little girl they found in me.

°•₀₍ⁿ₎₀•° ... °•₀₍ⁿ₎₀•° ... °•₀₍ⁿ₎₀•°

To Be

To feel so full with not a place to go. To be so ready not to be. Not to run, only to be me.

To be truly happy on my own time. To apply for a job everywhere I want. Not to cringe at the sound of my name. To have no one at all talk about my past. Only to have no one judging my life.

To be comfortable in my skin. To smile inside. To proudly look people in their eyes. To know I am given a chance. To be given a chance. To be looked at for me. To be happy to be me. To be me and be happy.

To not wonder if they know me. To not care because they don't. To know they don't, even if they think they do. To know my abilities and capabilities. To know my worth without any limits. Without any limits. Without these limits. To be me and be happy in my skin.

°•₀₍ⁿ₎₀•° ... °•₀₍ⁿ₎₀•° ... °•₀₍ⁿ₎₀•°

Choose Wisely

If I make one wrong mistake, I have a hard time facing things. I try not to face it, in return I mess up worse! I do not want to be a repeat, so many choices to be made.

I am trying to get this under control, I feel stuck with nowhere to go. I have these steps right in front of me, it's just at times I don't know where to begin. I must change my company, it's something I have been rudely hit in the face with.

The people I have chosen for friends, could care less about me in the long run! I must focus on school, work, and my daughter, doing this I will never regret! I must choose carefully the people around me, they must be examples of what my heart really is.

I care about others no matter what, I don't wish bad on anyone! It seems this is rare in this world, People only looking for what they can get from you. I may be alone for a while, but it's better than being around people who mean me no good.

°•₀ⓘ₀•° ... °•₀ⓘ₀•° ... °•₀ⓘ₀•°

In These Shoes

I sit right now and wonder how is it people are fake and cruel without love within? I guess that God just made me different, I would never change this life I'm living. I choose to love all those around me even when they don't truly see.

That's not the point and it doesn't matter what they think, my life and dreams shall always remain. Only God can change my world, I'm thankful and blessed no matter how life turns. I am a lover and sometimes I must fight but if I fight you better know my heart is right.

I could never be fake to myself putting the true me on a shelf. I really don't care who likes me or not, my life and choices are between me and God. I live for God, at least I try, so I will go to Heaven when I die. Also, because I want people around me to see my shining light does not come from me.

It's crazy but there are people who don't believe, I want them to know God and be set free! I even pray for those who claim they hate me, I love them and want what's best for them daily. It is hard sometimes to overlook their actions but look how Jesus did so why should it matter? I'm glad I choose to never grow cold, not that plenty of stories haven't been told.

That's just it, they just don't matter, for God Knows all truth and makes liars scatter! On my hard days I do slip up, I may get mad, I may even cuss. In the same breath I ask God to forgive, he knows this world is hard to live in. I calm back down, I pray and smile, people couldn't walk in my shoes, not even one mile!

°•o(j)o•° ... °•o(j)o•° ... °•o(j)o•°

Never Die

Watch the breeze blow the trees and shake each and every leaf. As the time of my life passes by I arrive at a place and sigh. Where am I? Have I learned to fly? I am not going to die! I am going to live, to give, to live eternally through God above.

This is real love. This love he gives all he asks is that you live. Live for him with all your heart. Then when your soul and body are apart, your soul will rise up to the skies. Therefore, really, you never die. In the end, tears may be shed, but know no soul who knows God is dead.

For they rest high above us all and on our angels We all can call. They love God as we do and one day we will see him too. For a soul who knows God will never die.

°•○⊙○•°   ...   °•○⊙○•°   ...   °•○⊙○•°

Sometimes

Sometimes life is so good, all the messages are understood. Sometimes life gets turned inside out, you don't have a clue what it's all about. Sometimes you could laugh forever, everything Seems to come together. Sometimes you could just give up, you seem to have had quite enough.

Sometimes a good friend is right there, you feel as though this life you'll bare. Sometimes it's as if no one cares, you then realize who wants to be there. Sometimes what you think is real is nothing more than what you want to feel. Sometimes when the sky is gray you must know there will be better days.

Sometimes when it seems bad, you see that your Life isn't so sad. Sometimes things happen for a reason even when you just can't see them. Sometimes when you want to give up, you realize that you've just begun.

°•○⊙○•°   ...   °•○⊙○•°   ...   °•○⊙○•°

To Know

To know why it is. To know how it feels. To know what to do, I want to be real. I know how it feels to be non-existent in my world, to wonder when someone is going to acknowledge my presence, my essence. No confidence instilled into an already insecure little girl.

What was to become of such a lonely little girl? What was going to happen to her as she grew? What could she do? She could be really quiet and not disturb others. She could try hard in school, but was it good enough? Yes, it was good enough, yes it was!

And now, more than ever, it was good enough! It is good enough! What was to become of such a lonely little girl? A woman with an understanding of life's hardships. A woman of strength and honesty, of pure goodness. A woman who can make anything happen with effort. A woman willing to give all she's got.

A woman who knows what truly will make her happy and complete, loving herself, it's all she needs! Her whole life falls into place when she sees who she really is. In the blink of an eye, it was all worth it.

If she can say she knows why things happened, she can change her outcome and ending. She doesn't have to simply let life run its course, she can take action and make choices for the good. She can break the cycle because she knows why!

°•○◍○•°   ...   °•○◍○•°   ...   °•○◍○•°

Your Truth

When the leaves start to turn, And the tears start to burn. The moment of truth hangs low. I have more strength then shows, although at times I have nowhere to go. In the shadows below the wind starts to blow.

Can I go? Do you hear me soul? How do we decide Our Fate when everything seems to be laid on our plate? Then a voice rings in my head! O child of mine haven't you listened? Turn to me if you feel broken! For, in the end your heart I can mend! I love you!

Transformation

To rake the leaves of another season gone. The leaves; some green, brown, yellow, or red. One thing is true all the leaves are dead. In the winter it gets cold, the leaves cannot live so I've been told. The snow covers the branches of the tree so beautifully.

Covering every part of the tree that has no leaves. It stays cold for quite some time, yet the tree is strong, it does not die. Soon enough spring will be, the snow will melt right off the tree. The sunlight will nourish the soul of the tree that has seen many seasons of this degree.

Once again, the leaves will begin to grow, as if a cold day the tree had never known. The leaves open spanning far and wide. You would not think these leaves could die. By Summer time the leaves begin to know. Soon enough they too will go.

°•o⊙o•°   …   °•o⊙o•°   …   °•o⊙o•°

My Delusions of Jezebel

Sometimes I have to contemplate why it is God gave me this fate. Why is it when we say goodbye a lot of times I want to cry? You hurt me, and you dog me out, I just don't know what that's about. I always waited for a real mother but seeing this makes me run for cover.

I want to just simply give up, because you make my life so rough. I've had to do so much alone when all I wanted was a loving home. Still, you choose to be so mean, I wonder if we're enemies? Are we family? Do you really care? Time after time it's up in the air.

Shouldn't a daughter know that she is loved? I shouldn't have to even give it a second thought. I question your love, and question again, then I feel loved for a little bit. Then, once again, it goes back to square one, frankly I'm feeling like my heart is done.

My eyes are burning, my soul is weary, I really wonder why you do this to me. Your first-born child, your only girl, did you even want me in this world? If so, why don't you cherish me, and love me like it's supposed to be? Because this right here is not real love, real love comes from God above.

It's pure, it's genuine, it sees no flaws, it loves with no conditions at all. My entire life all I ever wanted was you, but I never knew this is what you would do. I think the part that hurts the most is that sooner than later you will be a ghost. The child in me has longed for you, and now you are slowly dying too.

To add to that you flip and flop, but worst of all and at the top, you try to discredit me in front of my kids, you always have, and you always will. My own daughter looks at me different, when her mother was there and mine was missing. Now tell me how does this all work, how in the end I look like the jerk?

I know my kids love you dearly, but over and over you just don't hear me. You choose to taint them and baby them too, you secretly tell them bad things I do. I cannot continue to allow this to happen, I love my babies and I want this to matter. For you say that I am hard on them, but do you realize you put them through hell?

You make them choose which side to take, and their choices come from all that's fake. I just don't see any good in this, it's crazy that all you want is to win. I want them to be successful, you'll be happy with my day being stressful. No one can imagine my pain and grief, it feels as though half of me is a thief.

Somewhere deep inside of you is a person who just wants to be loved too. The difference is you just don't know, how to accept love or how to show. I guess I have to remember back, you have always been the one attacked. Or, just not loved as you should be, but knowing that I would think you'd love me.

°•○(J)○•°   ...   °•○(J)○•°   ...   °•○(J)○•°

Live Well

Life is not always the same at all, sometimes you soar, sometimes you fall. I have seen the good, I have seen some bad, I have been full of joy, I have been sad. One thing through it all that stays the same,

Father God's love is sovereign! During hard times we must remember, He gave us everything, even the stormy weather! The ups and downs, the good and bad, all things are a part of Father God's plan!

When going through times of hardship, when going through the unknown, the greatest gift we will ever have is the love that we can show! See, we never know what tomorrow holds,

We can get so caught up in ourselves. Loving those around us matters most, for we never know when to Heaven we each will go! So, just love others come what may, for one day your loved ones will go to Heaven above!

°•○◌○•° ... °•○◌○•° ... °•○◌○•°

Words

One thing I have seen time and again, saying negative things is not our friend. We get upset, we say hurtful things, we can't take them back for in the heart they ring. Why must there be anger and hate? If we have anger or hate how does love reign?

How do we say we love someone yet turn around and verbally assault them? I do know none of us are perfect, I also know real love is worth it! If we make a mistake and we fall from grace, I hope we could at the least say sorry.

Forgiveness is free, this is true, but let us acknowledge what we do. It goes so far to humble oneself, to swallow our pride and admit we were wrong. Otherwise, we leave room for hurt and pain, and really it only leaves room for Satan!

°•∘ⓘ∘•° ... °•∘ⓘ∘•° ... °•∘ⓘ∘•°

Deceived

Today I can't say why or how, I feel the way I do right now. Each day passes, and I wonder how I do it. You would think by now in sorrow I would drown, But, I am a hard person to hold down.

I am hated around this town; I won't let it keep me down! Through time I will be alright. For now, I need to end this night. My heart aches for something real;

Something I can truly feel. A real man to treat me right, and hold me through the lonely nights. Not a temporary fix, Or a quick pick.

No matter when or how I will find a sweetheart, He will be grateful to give me a new start. Until then, keep pushing, Me you're not using!

°•∘ⓘ∘•° ... °•∘ⓘ∘•° ... °•∘ⓘ∘•°

Loss

The legacy of loss, that was so long ago, was forced into your heart, and you cannot let it go. It is not your friend, and time will never heal, A truth you hold so close, A truth that seems so real.

So, hold onto the night, never let it go. The pain has cut too deep, will you ever know? For all the time that's wasted, All the years apart, there are many memories of you, Deep inside my heart. Our legacy lives on, as sad as that may be, it lives on in you, but it stops here with me!

°•ₒ₍ᵢ₎ₒ•° ... °•ₒ₍ᵢ₎ₒ•° ... °•ₒ₍ᵢ₎ₒ•°

Why

I feel so used, so powerless, with this power you are obsessed. My children suffer, and I do too, even your child and even you! Yet, you continue to self-destruct, thinking you show us love.

It is your choice to act this way and forever we will not stay. I've begged and pleaded, nothing works, so I resort to calling you negative words. Then, I am wrong and how could I all the while I am dying inside.

Do I enjoy the abuse? Does it seem I have grown immune? Immune to what hurts inside because my life has been a rollercoaster ride. I have four children who I love, and they must always come above. You've made it clear you will not change, I cannot be the one to keep taking the blame.

The end is near, I feel the roar, soon you will walk right out the door. I'll be left once again to fend for myself and no one wins. The kids get bounced from here to there and I am the only one who cares. Where are all those who love me the most, right now they all look like some ghosts. All I want is my family to work, right now it looks like nothing is certain.

°•○⊙○•° ... °•○⊙○•° ... °•○⊙○•°

The Message

A message, my message I send to all, On God's love you must call! This world deceives, hurts and leaves. Only in God you find true peace! So now you know who to turn to, don't ever feel useless, worthless, or old!

When lies surround you, He is the truth, he is beauty, he is pure! You could never measure up; Yet in his eyes you have always been enough, you've always had purpose, you have always been loved! He gave the world his only begotten son Jesus, All because   of his love for us!

°•○⊙○•° ... °•○⊙○•° ... °•○⊙○•°

I Must Go!

Isn't it crazy how amazing people can be, I think I'm in a maze with no ending. You say you love me, something you do not show, soon I know that I must go. You hurt and abuse me to the core, I just don't think I can take much more. I love you, oh yes, I do, but you cannot see this, and it makes me blue.

Time and again we fight and argue, right now I just don't know what to do. Four years we've been at this game, yet things just remain the same. We can't even see eye to eye, tell me why we shouldn't say goodbye. Give me a reason, one reason, that I should stay, our baby boy is what you say.

Truth be told, he is a reason to go, I do not want him thinking this is how love is shown. He ignores me because you show him that, he is a toddler, and this is so sad. You only see things that you want to see, all the while the picture doesn't include me. Let me go if you refuse to give, this is a way that I refuse to live.

The saddest part is throwing away my love, you will be upset when you realize it was. It was so real and true, but in your eyes, I am too good to love you. So, lose the love of your lifetime, because you're too busy living in the limelight. I cannot stay, I really must go, my love I have tried and tried to show.

What I get is rejection from you, sometimes you can be so cruel. Why, I ask, and do not know, then I realize I must go! Because your love you will not show, therefore, we will not grow so I must go. Why do I stay, myself I ask, my mind is mad at my heart's task?

One day I know I will have my share, who knows maybe I am already there. I try to hold on for change, but deep inside your heart stays the same and plays games. It just isn't fair to a heart so true, you can't appreciate me and this you've shown.

In the end don't be upset, you always want what you can't get. Crazy thing is you can have all of me, my heart, my soul, and my body. You do not see, and it is killing me! You won't love me, you just want my help, and you don't want to see me with anyone else.

°•o⋒o•° ... °•o⋒o•° ... °•o⋒o•°

Addicted to Abuse

Why? Why me? What did I do? You act as though you're just too cool. You go about not showing love, and then on me you push and shove. My heart I gave, a child too, none of this seems to matter to you.

So, here I am without my lover, to once again be a single mother. What, I ask, is left of my heart? Each time this happens I am torn apart. I know that I did not hurt you, I loved you and I loved you true.

You cheated, you lied, you made me cry. You moved on, you said goodbye. You didn't believe that I loved you; You couldn't see how that could be true. All this time, what have I been doing? You act as though we were just screwing.

You've lost it all, my love, our love. For what? Nothing will ever be above. We could have really had it all, But, you couldn't make that call. You couldn't even give in to your heart, Now, we will spend a lifetime apart.

°•o⊕o•°   ...   °•o⊕o•°   ...   °•o⊕o•°

Unconditionally

I love you unconditionally, no matter who you are or how you choose to be. I never say what you can't do, I only show my love for you. Not the you that you're destined to be, The you right here in front of me. Not the you I want you to be, the beautiful human in you I see. For we all have faults and things left to do,

When we look back we will know too. Every moment spent engrossed in selfish desires cost the most! Take a look at me, tell me, is it me you see? It is as if you are blindfolded, only listening to the voices in your head. I'd like to think those voices say, "I love you no matter what."

Because the truth is you can't show me when I'm gone! Looking back on life, Loving others is always right! We will never ever regret at all, A life lived loving unconditional!

°•o⊙o•° ... °•o⊙o•° ... °•o⊙o•°

Am I Alive

As I sit here all alone in a room full of people, it occurs to me that this wound is deeper. I need to speak, I need to talk, But, only one thing is in my thoughts! As days go by nothing seems to change, this world, to me, is so deranged!

I just seem to sit and stare, I never thought I would be there! I want to feel safe and secure, Reality says that could take years. Then, when things seem to be all better, I realize this will stay with me forever.

I must focus, I can't die inside, But, right now deep inside I cry. I thought that I was going to die, God saved my life yet still I cry. I'm sad, I'm scared, and I feel so alone, I feel that my relationship is gone.

This last straw broke the camel's back, Now, we just sit back and attack. When we need each other the most, we both put up walls and our love grows cold. My life has changed, so has our love, we need to hug, not push and shove.

°•o⊙o•°   ...   °•o⊙o•°   ...   °•o⊙o•°

How Long

I love you, yes this is true. I never tried to hurt you, I only wanted to be here for you. I've been here through good and bad I have stuck around, and mostly you've just let me down. Yet I stay not for one thing or another, But because you're the father and I'm the mother.

I see these boys their eyes light up, Whenever daddy comes to give them hugs. And me, my eyes swell up with tears, wondering how long this will go on because it's been years. Your fears should be long forgotten, you should only be afraid our love might go rotten.

Yes, I love you oh so very much, and yes, you have me with one single touch, But, I wonder as time creeps on, how long will I hang on? How long this time will I wait by the phone, even as time after time you don't call. I can wish and dream but still no reply, you act like loving me will cause you to die.

I love you still, and always will, but you don't feel this love I feel. So, let me go, just let me know I'm not the one you're loving, I'll be fine in due time I'll get into something. Men for me come with a price, a price I am done paying in my life. I could be sad or mad, but it's not worth the time.

I have things I plan to do, Sad to say with or without you. I'd like to know you'd be right there, but as you say you're everywhere. My mind is blown by what you have shown, and it can't be re-done. So, live your life as you wish and just know you are always missed.

°•o◯o•°   ...   °•o◯o•°   ...   °•o◯o•°

Soul Food

I am hungry o so hungry. I want some soul, yes, a side of soul. As I look in this room there is a giant hole, a half a person that has been stole. Who has done the stealing you ask? For this answer we must go back in the past.

I often long for what should of, could of, would have been, but never really was. I had a picture in my mind, but in reality, it was never us. To see, to feel, a love so unique it leaves you to ponder and really think deep.

Is a love so true and real going to end up being for you? Maybe dreams don't come true, and real true love is not me and you. But what if love was there to find? To search and seek that one of a kind. In due time love shows its face.

It has no sex, no color, no race. It's there and it is not going anywhere, no matter how much people just don't care. So please see it for exactly what it is; to love, to hate, to take, and to give.

°•o◯o•°   ...   °•o◯o•°   ...   °•o◯o•°

Foolish Love

What has happened in one second, I ask myself, Yet, the answer is not clear. Is it that I cannot hear? Those that are so dear. I do fear, have fear, hate fear. What do you fear? I love you near, I fear you far away. I don't want you to go, please stay.

It may be short as far as time, But, this love just continues to shine. If you don't see this heart of mine, you must truly be blind. My love for God, my love for us, this is much more than simple lust. Yes, making love is real, However, talking is something we both feel.

We get along, we both love hard, it's sad to think we may just part. So, for now, I don't, unless you make me, I won't. I love you and that's a fact, I wish I could put on an act.

°•○ⓘ○•°   ...   °•○ⓘ○•°   ...   °•○ⓘ○•°

Heaven Is Real

For you, for me, what do we do? I just don't know, is something new? I look around, I see not a thing, not a person, no one to blame.

I'm all alone in my pursuit of truth. It seems that people just don't want to know. They just live and don't care if they grow. I want to learn, I want to know.

Who loves me and who doesn't care if I go. I love too hard, I love too long. Why must I be this darn gone? I'm ready for love, can you hear me?

I'm waiting on you to truly see! In times like these I do wonder, Am I doing the right things for another? I feel so strong and yet so weak.

Why is it that I'm so darn meek? I look for signs, one way or the other, Yet I never know which road to discover. I'm sure one day I will know, Which side of the road, which way to go.

Until that time, I'm with my guy, the guy I'll go to when I die. My soul shall live forever indeed. My Father in Heaven knows me.

I only hope my loved ones are there; Or come one day so we can share, share life and love and be sincere. I know I will see Heaven one day, I also hope it's a long time away.

When I get there, I will shout hello, For I am sure there's people I know!

°•o℗o•°   ...   °•o℗o•°   ...   °•o℗o•°

Forgotten

Sitting here the tears I cry, nobody wants to say goodbye. Do these feelings really matter if our love only seems to clatter? We try to get by on love solo, but just how far will this love go? You say that I should be grateful, yet you are usually angry and hateful.

I'm so sick of your lack of understanding, you are just way too demanding. And yet in still you always say, "Because you see it only your way." It's funny that I've never heard, "My bad baby I'm acting absurd." I wonder if it's even possible to never ever reach an obstacle.

We both know this can't be true, not one is to blame, it's me and you! Our love fizzles with each sunset, no matter what I won't forget. Forget you not, I never could; I wonder if you even would? Would you miss me, would you care, if one morning I was no longer there?

Because I remember such a time our love was like a poetry rhyme. Never dull, never alone, always happy right at home. Now, it's like you hate my guts saying that it's all about trust. Do you hate me time tells all? In the end I refuse to fall. For I know what you do not, I am one in a million and I will never be forgotten!

°•○◎○•° ... °•○◎○•° ... °•○◎○•°

Legions

In your eyes I see demise, to the occasion of betrayal you quickly rise. You don't know love, you only know pain, so in this life you are all about gain. You've been hurt, you've been abused, you know very well how it feels to be used. Your heart is burdened, your eyes full of tears, you've gone on this way for many years.

I try to show you how to love, to live each moment for the big man above. Everyone around you is a target for abuse, I want to know what is the sense or use? What do you gain by hurting others? It could be your mom or even your brother. You envy all, you have no shame, everything in life is merely a game.

See, in your heart it's cold and black, you are always on the attack. You look at people who are genuinely happy and you pick them apart as emotional and sappy. You call them fake, you hate their life, but truth be told you see their light. You see something in them you wish you could be, but all you truly need is to set yourself free!

Free from lies, free from stories, you make stuff up just not to be boring. Yet, you don't realize, and you don't see the reason I am happy is because I am being true to me! I do not care what others think, I am the one who chooses to dream! I love to see other people happy and, in my opinion, this is not sappy!

I just don't understand why you are this way, I fear for you because one day God will make you pay! See, life is far from a game, what you do to others you should be ashamed! So, I will pray that you see the truth, everything you need God put in you!

°•o◯o•°   ...   °•o◯o•°   ...   °•o◯o•°

My Baby Girl Grew Up

That moment you realize your daughter is all grown up. I sit, and I question if I showed her enough love. Did I teach her what is most important in this life? I know if I didn't I surely tried. I thought life was over when you were first born, I was 16, alone, and deeply torn. It didn't take long for me to see, what a precious gift God had given me. God blessed me with you and changed my soul. So live, love, and be bold! You are such a wonderful young lady, I thank God you are my baby! No amount of years, tears or pain could change what he gave me, Love remains.

Your chubby cheeks and bright blue eyes, they changed my life and stopped my demise. Now, don't get me wrong, I made plenty of mistakes, as you well know life gives and it takes. I hope that you see how special you are, and what unique place you have in my heart. Yes, I would give anything to return to the time, when you were so tiny, and your love was all mine. Truth is, I cannot ever go back, right about now I am feeling bad!

Being so young, I thought I missed out, but having you is what life's truly about. I'm proud to say you are my daughter, But I wonder are you proud I am your mother? In life and in love forgiveness is so important, it opens those doors that we left to lie dormant. So, I ask you today, as I sit, and I cry, can you please forgive me? Only God knows why! Why I let men abuse me and overlooked you, while you sat there crying, so sad and so blue.

Now I can only hope and pray, that you understand what I'm trying to say. This life is not promised, our days are all numbered, Often, I find myself to sit and to wonder. What would I do, if I could go back? Well, I'd love you and love you and that is just that! As we both know, only forward we go, But, with these lessons we are pained to know.

I love you so much, your brothers too, I know in my heart you know this is true! One day, when I'm gone, only memories will remain, I can only pray that it is not only pain. I hope you remember laughter, joy, and smiles, And, remember baby girl it's only for a while. My life goes on through my beautiful babies, I thank God for these babies he gave me. To hold, to have, and to love forever, this stands true no matter the weather.

°•o℗o•°   ...   °•o℗o•°   ...   °•o℗o•°

Man Made

The man you are is real to me. I see the man you want to be. The man always lying next to me, making sure we are happy and free. I love you for who you are, Without the car, money, or power.

That man comes from so much strength, this one paragraph could never explain. I look in your eyes and I see, this man looking back at me. Nothing or no one else, just him. The chances of me leaving are slim. One touch and my body goes crazy.

You don't have to do much to amaze me. I would be with you until the end, till one of us are cold and dead. But, do you know what's in my heart? Do you know I never want to part? I wonder   if you really know, if you do you should let it show.

°•o℗o•°   ...   °•o℗o•°   ...   °•o℗o•°

Lie and Wait

These feelings harbor, they lie and wait, to see tomorrow and find their fate. I witnessed your shadow, a door closed tight, I just don't see how it could ever be right.

I realize that time changes everything, there really is no one to blame. I visualize what God has planned, and I am thankful I'm not with that man. I waited long enough for nothing, but maybe I learned how to be loving.

The trials and truths they crash like thunder, the plan I had goes tumbling under. Out comes a woman so strong and true, a woman who no longer needs you.

The hard times come with two choices to make, I can learn from my wrongs or keep making mistakes. My choices tell of my future life, will I continue to do what's right? Never settle for less than the best and say goodbye to all the rest.

°•o◍o•° ... °•o◍o•° ... °•o◍o•°

My Plans

Anytime he calls I am on cloud nine, I'm thanking God right now for me and mine. We been through hell and back again. In the end God knows we win. So thankful for the little things, Like smiles and flowers and wedding rings.

God says it's time for my destiny. Now, all we need is for you to be free. I'm waiting, I'm waiting, quite patiently. I know how good you will be to me. You always loved me, it never stopped, Now look, just look at what we got.

Not a show, not fake or plastic, Just real true love and it's everlasting. I love you boo, I always have. Now that you know, you can't be sad. For God has blessed you with your queen, I'm right here, just look, it's me.

I also have been blessed with my king, to have and hold just like a dream. But, as I said it's all so real, Love and joy and hope we feel. I thank you Jesus for my best friend, For I know our bond will never end.

Too Much

I am here, you are there, this doesn't seem to be real fair. Then, I remember God has the plan, we all could use a helping hand. I fear that time can do so much, all I want is your touch. When the nights are lonely, and the days forever last, some day we can say this is all in the past. At this moment it doesn't sound likely, but trust and believe it all will be! I just don't know if we can make it, I believe if we pray enough, we can be great.

I see the devil trying to attack us, instead of worrying we must not fuss. There is so much put on my shoulders, the weight is so heavy like a huge boulder. I am frustrated at all I do by myself, everyone at times needs some help. Why am I blamed for everything? Choices, chances, consequences. It's crazy when your family already has your Life planned out, but even crazier is when they plan for you to fail.

°•○(i)○•° ... °•○(i)○•° ... °•○(i)○•°

Selfish Heart

Just when you think it's over, your pain has come and gone, something trips you up, leaving you to be torn. How could your love be true? How could you really care?

When all I've done is plead and beg, for you to just be there! I'm an adult now and I would think, I wouldn't feel this hurt and pain. Maybe it's better if you're not in my life anymore, it might just be my last resort!

I've tried to close the door, I've tried to make you see. You look out for one person, that one person is not me! Now what is just is, and whys don't count. One day you'll regret it all, Or, maybe you will never figure it out.

°•○◎○•°   ...   °•○◎○•°   ...   °•○◎○•°

Soul Ties

The slightest touch from you leaves me spinning in the room. I don't know how this goes, how this flows we don't really know. I know you well and care a lot, maybe we will be together, maybe not.

As time goes on my love grows strong, it is only growing stronger, is that wrong? I wonder at times, will my heart break but, who cares because it already aches. I can't forsake a love so real, a love only few people will ever feel.

I can't turn my back on you, you won't go away, will you? If it is true how much you care, then just be real and be there. If you have doubts or are unsure bad times we can get through and endure. No matter what, until the end of time, my heart will beat for you, and I will want you to be mine.

°•○◯○•° ... °•○◯○•° ... °•○◯○•°

My Cries Are Heard

I am at a loss, life only costs. I doubt my life will ever be the same, my question is: Am I to blame? My mind wonders, I sit and think did I possibly have too much to drink? Did I somehow give the wrong idea? When I said no did I really mean it? I hung around him, I chose it right? I didn't struggle, I didn't fight...

I only wish I could go back to that night! I never would have drunk so much, I never would have let him touch. I fell asleep but when I awoke my life to me was a scary joke. I have thought for days to end it all, but then I hear God's mercy call! He says to me "It happened, it's over, you must move on" Yet I don't feel that I am that strong.

He replies, "No my child, you are not, but I will carry you, I have the plot." I have a plan, I need your help and sometimes it includes a whelp. It includes some tears and overcoming fears, but through it all I am here. Your life was set the day you were born, I know at times you have been torn. You have been hurt, you have been burned, but don't you see the others turn?

They look at you, they see your smile, it helps them for a little while. The love you show each day on Earth is my gift to others, directly through you. Don't fret, don't worry, it will be okay. I know all he did, and I promise he will pay. You don't need revenge, anger, or hate. I have it covered, you'll see one day. The bottom line my child, you see, is truly you are working for me.

You are not bad, you are so good, I need that to be understood! Not by this world, or anyone else, I need for you to know yourself! I know this life has been more than you can bare, I took you through it to get you there. Where is there you may be asking, I will show you and it's everlasting! My child, I need you please don't give up, although I know you've been through enough.

My plan for you on Earth is hard, I won't Pretend it's a game of cards! Yet through everything I have taken you through the test of love remains in you! I am so proud you are this way and I promise you if you just pray; I will give you everything you need, I will never let you down, you can trust in me! Many others hurt just like you, their life is different, they walk different shoes.

But deep inside it's pain they feel, pain you Know is all too real! I'm not sure you Understand just how much you can help them! You listen, you hug, you share my love; these things make my heart full. The rewards for you are great and many, nothing on this Earth will ever be satisfying! I know your heart longs for love and I continue to send it like a dove.

It may come soft, it may come slow, but I need for you to continue to grow. One day you'll be in a perfect place, a place filled with love, mercy and grace. Don't give up waiting on that day, I have too much for you to do this day! I love you more than words can say but I know you know this anyway!

°•○⑩○•°   …   °•○⑩○•°   …   °•○⑩○•°

Blessings in Disguise

I can't put a name on the way I feel. Right now, this wound is all too real! I feel that day just creeping up. Right now, I don't feel tough enough. My scar reopened and now it's bleeding. Forgiveness is what I know I'm needing!

This is where my ball stops rolling. It's deep down inside this grudge I'm holding. I don't know where to begin to forgive. I mean, after all, he doesn't deserve it. But I quickly remember forgiveness is not for him. It's for me to let go and have peace from within.

It may seem so simple to someone observing, but unless you've been through it you don't know the hurting. Something like this stays with you forever. Yet it doesn't have to be all bad, the storm you can weather! God will always do what he promises, He will show you how to get on with it!

Get on with your life, be happy, keep growing. Soon enough, other people you are showing. You are giving them what they need to move on. You're sharing your wisdom and making them strong! So, you have been blessed in disguise, God promises that until your body dies!

°•○⑩○•°   …   °•○⑩○•°   …   °•○⑩○•°

Could Be

I could be lost, exhausted, and done but I remember Jesus and to him I run! At times I allow negative to rule my day when all I have to do is pray! The enemy is good at his deception, yet when we call on Jesus the enemy runs!

We are all human and God knows this well, but we have the choice of Heaven or Hell! Each moment of every day we must remember to keep on praying! God does not care where we have been, I consider him my closest friend!

He doesn't bend, he will never break, he will never hurt you or be fake! He simply wants what is best for you, he sent his son Jesus to die for you! He will never deceive, he will never cheat, you see with Abba the enemy is already beat!

Yet we are flesh and flesh is weak, the enemy knows us, our weaknesses and strengths! He wants us all, not just a few, please ask yourself: does the enemy have you? We must remember his job is to destroy and defeat, he wants us on him to rely and retreat!

I have been destroyed and devastated, yet because of Jesus I am being remade! I thank you Lord, I always do, even when I forget it is you that I am next to! When I am weak you carry me, when I am strong it is your strength! The troubles of life can be a load, sometimes the path is just not shown.

I pray for answers day and night, at times I receive them at times it's a fight. I try so hard to do as you would do, it's easy to say but hard to wear your shoes.

The enemy comes to kill and seeks to destroy, he begins this mission when we are little girls and boys.

Yet Jesus defeated Satan's every plan, he did it for every single woman and man! I will admit it is hard sometimes; you know God's here and yet you cry. The pain this world can cause a heart is as a bow and arrow straight to my heart.

God gives us weapons of his defense like breastplates , shoes and a crown of righteousness. I'm learning day by day that even in pain, God brings the sunshine after all the rain. Even in struggle, heartache, and pain he makes a way for us to shine once again!

Thinking of life this way helps us keep peace and joy throughout each day. We may not know why things come about, but still praise Jesus, yes, scream and shout! Thank you, Jesus, I thank you so very much; there is so much power in the grace of your touch.

I sit here in the middle of storms and pain, yet I can deal with it all just calling your name. The more I choose to call on you, in moments of weakness or not knowing what to do, I feel closer and closer my soul to you; the world has no cure, but you do!

You remind me of your divine timing, that it may rain but your son is always shining. It doesn't have to be a focus, pain that is, because every life every heart is truly his. He knows what he is doing when we have no clue, he knows the unseen, something we cannot do!

He loves us in a way we can't even comprehend, it has no beginning and it has no end. I know from my own life it is not easy to follow Jesus, he knows our hearts and our effort he sees it. Not one single thing he does not know, so when he tells you to do something just go!

Go out each day with a smile upon your face, knowing he walks with you giving you grace. I have learned to keep the focus on him, as I already know in him I win! Walking with him in my imperfect effort, it gives God joy, his heart it blesses!

It also takes pain and turns it to joy, peace out of chaos, and sunshine from storms! It makes us human to feel and hurt, it makes it all better to know it's all worth it. I must remember all the moments of suffering you endured, deep suffering I couldn't go through!

Life for me cannot possibly be even close to all the suffering you had to see! You were human, you were flesh, yet you sinned not and overcame death! In this victory I rejoice I rejoice I rejoice!

More and more I only long for your voice! Your will your plan is all I want, in struggle or in joy it is all about you God! We got to know nothing is easy, yet our souls doing your will are deep down pleased!

You turn bad to good as in Romans 8:28, so no matter what we see it will eventually be great! So, have faith and be encouraged, you can trust in God's every single word! When the world brings you to your knees, stay there and pray and you will   be relieved! Just know! Just know, he has you in his hand, and trust and believe his plan for you is grand!

Be You

As I lay in bed right now I think of how my life turned around. I wonder where my heart would be if Jesus never rescued me. He takes my pain and in exchange he fills my days with bright sun rays. If I could tell the world just how I feel I would say one word: loved!

God wants us to be full of joy and totally set free, in laying my life down I am finding me. I find myself truly amazed for his love is revealed to me in many ways. I could focus on what has already past or I could focus on making his love last. In the end we all want love, we all crave it, deep down in our souls!

If God is on your team you can trust you have been redeemed! All the things in your past can go away and never come back. Human beings tend to think, we think too much and falter God's dreams. He dreams for us to have his love so deep that everyone around knows he set us free!

He wants us firm and, in his word, and in return we shall never burn! There will be times when things look bleak but faith in God makes problems look meek. I tell you this as he tells me because he wants us all to be set free. Not one, not some, but all of us he cares for and he deeply loves!

Low and behold when I am called home, I will have broken every mold! Only because of Jesus, I was able to rise above! Above the noise of this world, above the hurt of a little girl! Choose what you may, decide what you wish, but I know the truth and I came to share it!

°•°o(i)o•°   ...   °•°o(i)o•°   ...   °•°o(i)o•°

What Will You Choose

Tell me why, can we ask ourselves? Why does everything have to come to this? People have so much hate, it hurts for me to even say. I go about my life each day, I try to live for love. I want more people to try it and see just what love does. Love can carry us Oh so far, way past where we currently are.

If I could change the world somehow, I'd ask for love right here and now! People think I am awfully crazy, they look at me and they're amazed. See I choose to love every time, this love I share is not really mine. I've asked for God to keep my heart pure, I asked God to make my love endure. Through pain and struggles, through time alone, I turn to God all on my own.

I can see why people do what they do, in this world we have all been abused. They have been hurt in many ways and they didn't choose love after all those days. Sometimes their hurt feels like my own, it's not mine and this I know. I just want them to feel better, to see the rainbow in stormy weather.

This is how I know I am special, I also know I am successful. In every day I live I choose, to see all the love through the abuse. That in itself is complete success, just look at my past I could be a mess. I have lived through quite a lot but I look at all that I have been taught. God needs me here, this I do know, to shine his light for me to show.

One thing I know it is not me, I don't take credit for all others see. He blessed me with a special gift, he told me how to love and give. I could be rich with money and wealth, but even better what I have inside myself! No doubt I have my bad and sad days, days I just want to lock myself away. But on those days the enemy wins, I never want for the devil to grin.

So once again I pick myself up, God says to do it, go show that love! In the end all that really matters is all the love I can spread and scatter! I can't forget all I have been through, but God can make me feel brand new. For me, that's better than a pot of gold, he's always there, my hand he holds. But let me tell you all my friends, he is there for you too, his hand he will lend.

Just trust me, you can see my life, you could look at the bad, see all the strife. But then have hope in all you do because God can help, he's there for you too! I'm not extra special, he is not all mine, he gives his love on all to shine! I'm asking you just try and see, the way I love it's God not me! I want for you to feel this love and it only comes from God above!

Can't you try, other things have failed, in his love I promise you will prevail. I won't go on in begging you, in the end only you can choose. I can say that you will always win if God's love is in your heart within. I'm done, I'll go, but one last thing; if you don't choose God the devil reigns.

To My Children

To my children I want you to know, in God's love I want you to grow. I know I'm not perfect and things can be hard, but in all you do allow God to play a part. I've tried my hardest to show you this, to hug you and love you, your face I kiss. I know there must be things I missed.

I love you dearly, I truly do, my life seems meaningless when I'm without you. I know God gave me you for a reason, I just want to be sure to please him. I hope and pray I raise you right, I have put up one heck of a fight. I may get mad and I may yell, but I just want you to be successful.

In time I hope you see my intentions, to be your parent and have a friendship. Right now, you're all doing well, considering the times I myself have fell. Through everything you may go through, just know God is right there with you. I don't know what else I can say, but love, live, learn, laugh, and pray.

You all have something you can offer, a gift God gave you, so you can prosper. Use it wisely, use it well, or life can be a living hell. When I've raised you and you are grown, I hope you have faith all on your own. If I can only give you this, then there is nothing I have missed.

I love you more than words can say, I hope you know this anyway. So, smile a lot and pray even more, remember God may close some doors. Only he has the plan, just have faith and hold his hand.

°•ₒ◎ₒ•° ... °•ₒ◎ₒ•° ... °•ₒ◎ₒ•°

Shock And Awe

I am officially in a place of shock and awe! I never really took the time to pause! I kept pressing through all the loss! So, Jesus could surely redeem his lost! I found a place of peace and grace! Then Father God put light upon my face!

I continued to praise the only name! The only name whose blood kills shame! I began to see a destiny for me! A destiny which included a queen! I then began questioning all things, that in 37 years had happened to me! I saw Father, his hand sovereign! I realized, my soul, he was always holding! I can thank Jesus a billion times! Even more, I must show him with my life! Some say that I am crazy!

Yet, the God in me is always amazing! I am sold out, yes, addicted to Jesus! He died to forgive all my sins! I cannot stop talking about him! I want everyone to see they are forgiven!

°•ₒ◎ₒ•° ... °•ₒ◎ₒ•° ... °•ₒ◎ₒ•°

Never Alone

I am in a room physically alone, Yet, all around me I feel the holy ghost! How precious, how rare, just call on sweet Jesus, he is already there. Do not worry for Jesus cares, He came from Heaven to be here! He came only for all of us, He didn't want the fall for us! So, I praise you, I thank you sweet Jesus, for saving us from our own mess!

°•○(ι)○•°   …   °•○(ι)○•°   …   °•○(ι)○•°

I Found Jesus

Sometimes it seems that God is mean, but really, he's simply awesome. Mankind really can't just understand things that are totally rotten. When going through these hurtful things it seems God is not around. Truth be told his love is bold and it just must be found.

Through hurt and pain, thunder and rain, his love is there, it always remains. The reason I can loudly proclaim this is all because of the scars on Jesus' wrists! He died for man to understand that God's love is real. The pain we all go through at times is nothing compared to what Jesus had to feel.

In his life he was not rewarded, he was always abandoned, and his truth distorted. If he can endure and go through all that, then we must hold on to his plan. No one said life would be easy, the devil's ways are very sleazy. But, when we choose to walk in Jesus' shoes, our life becomes more win than lose. I myself have seen enough, I've seen the awful, the terrible, the rough. How would I appreciate the beautiful times without some rain?

God allows all kinds of things to bring us closer to his place. His place of peace and love and dreams. He has a plan for each and every man. I have realized our plans will fail, it's just that simple, only his prevail. This is where we each come in, to decide what he wants from us deep within.

For within us all he put everything we need, He did not put hate, jealousy, or greed. When we witness these characteristics first hand, we must have faith and understand, the place where all evil things come from is not the man from up above! He gives us love, hope, and peace, He gives us all we really need!

So, don't be discouraged or too unhappy, when we make plans God begins laughing. It's when we seek what he wants and needs the blessings come like a stampede. Don't get me wrong, when we put him first it simply means we are no longer cursed. It doesn't mean life won't be hard, it doesn't mean it won't leave scars.

What it does mean for you and I is we never Truly have to die. While we are here on God's green earth we can be thankful for our rebirth. We should rejoice even in the worst of storms, it's in these times we are being transformed, if you believe and have faith, you will end up amazed.

God will turn the bad to good, he will use it however he should, make you see what needs to be done, but in these times, you may want to run. Don't you do it, don't you quit, just live just love and always forgive. I promise if you do these things you will be blessed beyond your dreams.

See, people seem to have forgotten because this world they have gotten lost in. The worldly things are not of God, seek higher and think bigger, it is your job. He has a task for each of us but how can we see it if we never trust? Just know through life, the good and bad, it's all for him and don't be mad.

Keep on loving to love some more, don't let your heart be a closed door. You may be hurt at times it's true, but at least you did all you could do. To love each person on this earth and show them they're loved beyond their hurts. Love comes straight from God himself, so when you find it share in that wealth.

No money or power could ever compare to the way it feels to show someone God cares. It's hard for man to understand what he himself cannot see, Therefore, God needs us all, including you and me. Even if we touch one person a day, slowly we can wipe the sadness away. You may say I am stupid or crazy, but the truth is I know God is amazing!

A time or two someone lent a hand, this is how I can understand. So, lend a hand, let your help be known, it's ironic how your mind will be blown. We don't know the ways in which we're made, we are simply living for this day. Seeing the peace, seeing the love, it fits us each just like a glove.

When we act on our gut and help, then we will know all about wealth. Wealth of the heart and of the soul, the never- ending filling of your spiritual bowl. And, such it pours on those around, oh my oh my here's where Jesus is found!

°•○ⓝ○•°   ...   °•○ⓝ○•°   ...   °•○ⓝ○•°

Message

I know it's hard, don't forget I was there. As hard as it is, my life you could never bare! Find strength in this when spreading my word; To pity yourself then seems absurd! For to suffer is to be like me and very few will ever see! So, instead feel privileged to suffer like me. For truly you are chosen for my glory!

I know it doesn't seem logical, just look back and be the prodigal! That's what you are, and what you have always been! In me, you know, you have a true friend! It may have taken a long time to find me, but please don't worry about one single thing!

For God is love and love is God! I am so thankful I know this now! I try to love in every way, in everything, on every day; When it's hard I choose to pray, see we all have choices to make each day! I choose you Jesus and I am glad I do! Now, I just want for everyone else to have you too!

°•o⊙o•°   ...   °•o⊙o•°   ...   °•o⊙o•°

Jesus Heals

I'm feeling full, I need to write. I don't know what it is tonight. I feel the need to share my story, I think God wants my testimony. When I think of sharing it with people, I get shy, it's not easy to do. I could do it if no one knew that it was me all I've been through. But, I think that is the point, he wants me to share so he can anoint.

He needs me to be cleansed, to come to grips with my past and begin to mend. That is not all that he wants, he needs people to see his heart in me flaunt. That, for me, is something hard, it requires me to put down my guard. I do know the things God needs are usually not very easy for me. But, look around! People every day choose to hate and go their own way.

They choose to be in their own prison, God has made this my first business! I don't know when and I don't know how but I do know on this I vow; One day, I will share my life, with everyone who is alive. My story shall reach the depths of people, I don't know how but I know it will!

I could say that I may be embarrassed, I may even get a little harassed. But, it's all for God, not for me, he needs for the whole world to see. One person can go through the most and be healed through the Holy Ghost. I'm excited but also, afraid, look at all the bad choices I've made. Then God says "That's the key, I love you anyway, and I set you free!

I need for people who doubt in me to see I love them and set them free! You sharing your story can help them see, you've been through hell but trusted me! It says a lot that you have faith, you could be miserable or horribly changed!

Yet, you chose me every time, I need for this to be on their minds! So, don't be shy, don't be timid, I will show them with me they can win! By their victory, you win too, because it started within you! I know you want to help these hurting people so just relax I've got work to do!"

Chain Breaker

To break every chain, what will remain? I know that you may wonder this very thing. Yet and still I choose Jesus, yes Lord you. Jesus, only your name and your ways will do. I have tried it all, now I rest in you, But Lord it hurts I cry for your truth.

You feed me every little thing I need, you keep me in a place of perfect peace. You comfort me in every time of need, I thank you Jesus, my life I give indeed. Many tears I have painfully shed, But, I am quickly reminded of the blood that you bled!

Lord at times I feel I can't go on, thank you for reminding me victory is already won. The road might be long, there might be suffering, But I came, your truth, to bring running. So, off I go Bible in hand, wherever you may lead, any place known to man. Father I shall always be unafraid, For, you are with me so who are they? You've shown, and you've proven time and again, you reign sweet Jesus, in you I win!

°•₀ⓜ₀•° ... °•₀ⓜ₀•° ... °•₀ⓜ₀•°

One Day

That moment when you realize even in your mistakes God always finds a way. He made you and he knows the end from the beginning. In times of trouble and turning to flesh, we can see that in him we must rest. If it were not for hard times and trials, there would be no room for his smiles.

I think of this and know it's true, the love he shares with me and you. It's real, it's bold, there is no other; with grace and love he comes to smother. He continues to love us when we don't love ourselves, he shows us how we should really feel. He only wants for you what is good, and this is sometimes misunderstood.

We trick ourselves into believing and for that reason we have been deceiving. Who we deceive may come as a surprise but in our hearts is where it lies. Being true to my Father is a process I want to prosper! I want God to know that he is my keeper and what is for me is whatever he pleases!

Anytime I try without him, it seems that something is forgotten! I fall and try to get up, but God must be my only crutch! I can't rely on this world's cures, this life I must with him endure! For in the next my soul can rest and in Heaven it will be at its best!

I have to look at life this way or else my mind will be led astray! For it is easy to be done simply wanting to have a little fun! What I have learned from life so far is God will meet us right where we are! In times when we want something other than his love we must once again search deep above!

There is no silver lining in this world, the enemy wants our souls' boys and girls. For if we live for what we want, our destiny's will never truly be sought. We learn this through God's only son who gave his life so that we live on. In life and death, we are the same when God's love in us remains.

The hurt, the pain, the shame is real, but Jesus made it start to heal. I just don't feel the same anymore, I could never shut this open door. I want to share for all to see the love that God has put in me. So, I go on this road alone but not really, not deep in my soul.

For there is a love that could never be erased, it could never be forgotten, it could never be replaced. Time and time again this love shall win until there is no more life in my sin! I pray that day is not far away as thus far it all could be replaced. One day can change anything if that one day on Calvary changed you and me.

°•o◎o•°   ...   °•o◎o•°   ...   °•o◎o•°

Mustard Seed

Lord Jesus Father God, no words could explain how I feel right now! Thank you, Daddy, for everything, you always mount me up on eagle wings! I trust you Abba, I truly do, So, my every moment is all about you! The challenges come, no doubt in this, but you only allow them for a little bit.

Time and again you rescue me, Time after time I feel more and more peace! More and more love, hope, joy, and relief, your perfect ways, they rest on me. I only want what you want Father, My faith is strong, stronger than ever!

When I pray for your will to be done, I don't know what I pray for, but I have faith in your son! Papa truly I don't know at all, what may come or where I shall go!

But I do know it is all in your hands, I do know you have a set plan!

I believe because Jesus died for love, I know my heart is safe in his love! So, on you Abba I trust and trust, knowing in righteousness I could never go wrong!

Fear

Where does it arise? Is it something deep inside? Or, does it go with shame or pride? This walk with king Jesus is far from easy, yet to each soul it is immeasurably pleasing. I see fear as the enemy's king, through fear he reaps havoc on everything! He stops us, if we allow, in doing things God says to do now. Saints, that is it, Fear is holding back God's gifts. I pray each soul reading this will make huge Waves for sweet King Jesus!

°•○◌○•° ... °•○◌○•° ... °•○◌○•°

Flesh

There is no time for selfish things, selfish ways, or selfish dreams. My time has come to look above and spread around this awesome love! Jesus died for all of us, not for himself, in this we trust. He chose to come down to earth and make it so our lives have worth!

When life in this world is done, we can live on through God's only begotten son. He gave his life long before those days on the cross, and he was called nothing but a loss. Most religious men gave Jesus grief and kept lying about him with no relief.

Jesus loved them anyway and called for others to follow what he laid. Jesus himself searched for the souls that needed him the very most. He did not judge, he did not boast, he still wanted those forgotten souls.

When times are rough, and the storm has come just know in him shines bright the son; The brightest days you will ever have, the saddest moments seem so glad. Now I know I can never be hurt again, at least not as I was way back when.

I didn't always know this love, I didn't believe in Jesus above. The day I realized that he was real, that he was something I could feel, I started to put aside my own life and do what I know is right. I have always had these crazy thoughts of great success and at all costs.

I just never knew that it was real, but now I know God helps me heal. He opens my eyes to truth and makes me impossible to be moved. In hardships is when he is restoring our faith, our love and hope can't be erased!

So, when times are at the very worst, just praise Jesus knowing you're not cursed. For his love is all we need, even when our flesh sows different seeds. We can choose to live in life through his spirit or live in death through our own flesh.

°•○◌○•° ... °•○◌○•° ... °•○◌○•°

My Flesh May Fail, You Never Will

Lord, I am in a quiet place of awe and sadness. I am experiencing events I never saw coming yet I am at a complete peace, knowing everything is your doing! I feel as though you warned me ahead of time, I just didn't listen and went ahead with this plan of mine.

Now I see faithful I will be to only you Lord! Flesh and blood may fail me, but you never will! Where people hurt me, betray me, leave me, judge me and be human, your love is supernatural and always there for me! Even when I don't call on you, you are still right here with me and all is well.

You lead the way, so I am sure my future is bright, Now I walk by faith and not by sight! I know You have my calling and my back, there is no such thing as coincidence! No matter what, your plan is the best, even if I must forsake all the plans I had before this!

°•○◐○•° ... °•○◐○•° ... °•○◐○•°

Grace

As I face the cold suddenly windy and blistering day, I remind my heart to keep first my faith. The days are long, and sleep is short, no time to waste thinking about remorse. I must be alert and cast down negative thoughts, Otherwise, my soul has a price to be brought.

There are many times I am ready to give in, Then I remember in the end we win! My flesh crawls, my face leaks with hurt and sin, I still stand firm, our Lord Jesus Christ I'm in! The enemy knocks, oh yes again and again, he comes through women, he comes through men.

He seeks to kill, and to destroy, Everyone God chose to employ. We must resist, we must flee quick, otherwise we are a sinking ship! Little by little, inch by inch we give in, before we realize our life is full of sin. So, stand tall, rejoice, the future is bright!

There is joy in the morning for those tears at night! I promise, I swear, it is worth the fight, you will never feel better than doing what's right! Your strength will soar on eagle wings evermore, you never even touch the floor.

God has you in his graceful care, So, this world could have you anywhere! We may see damage, abuse, or pain, Yet, we know there is sunshine after the rain! So, be encouraged, walk in peace, and love, real love, you will come to meet!

°•o₍ı₎o•° ... °•o₍ı₎o•° ... °•o₍ı₎o•°

Sifted

I feel like Peter being sifted as wheat, most days as of lately I barely eat. My soul is grieved, my heart skips beats, not knowing what to do, nothing is seen. I know Abba Father you are in charge, I know everything is in your power! I feel forsaken, yet I know I am not, I know I am in the will of God.

I had the most incredible summer, I was in pure joy of the Lord. I heard your voice as you said so much, it was as if I was right with you God. Now, I feel so unsure of my life, you say be still, don't go left or right. What happens next Abba, I don't know, nowhere to turn and nowhere to go!

I trust you, no doubt, I trust you, I just really don't know what to do! The revelations are so far away right now, I ask myself when, why, and how? I need your strength and guidance Lord, I can't do anything until you give me the word!

All I keep hearing is be still my child, yet the world is in chaos completely running wild! How can I save anyone if I am stuck, yet I am in this position just listening to you God! Please Lord help me to know who I am, help me to come to understand! I am so unsure of what comes next, I know this life is one big test! I only want to do what you tell me to, I know I always must trust in you! I am so preoccupied with what comes next, please Lord God give me your rest.

Show me the way each minute each day, I have never in my life felt this way. Many tests I have been through, do you find me worthy of your will? Why am I so afraid of the unknown, my faith should be growing as I read the Bible!

°•○◑○•° ... °•○◑○•° ... °•○◑○•°

Just Rest

As I wait and wait some more, I feel as if I have closed a door. There is no way to turn back, only forward I must track. I know God only puts on us so much, but I feel I have had more than enough! I am overflowing with stress but why?

I need my faith and a deep sigh! Everything is in his plan, I know, yet sometimes I wonder where will I go? What will I do? How will I live? Maybe myself I must forgive! It is so hard to let your mistakes go, we must leave them in the past or the pain never ends!

It's sad how we can feel so overwhelmed, so at the end, with nothing left to give. Really, we just need a little love from ourselves to feel better. So, when you're feeling that you have lost and you're down and out at all costs, look in the mirror and say to yourself "I love you and I am on the mend."

For all you have done, good or bad, cannot compare to your future God has planned! I am so ready to be stable and then I realize I am already able! Time-time-time- is the key, no one can change it, not you or me! You may say you want time to hurry but first your pain you must endure it! So, when you feel there's nothing left, just remember, you are at you best!

°•₀◖◗₀•° ... °•₀◖◗₀•° ... °•₀◖◗₀•°

My Salvation

I know that you have great plans for me, it's just at times I wish I could see. My faith has grown, I know I am known, Time and time again you have let this show. I thank you for your faithful love, And I will praise you no matter what! I am in a place where I don't know what you want of me. I am on a hill but the other side I cannot yet see. I know without a doubt you have good planned for me, So, I continue to be on my knees.

I pray my life is pleasing to you, for at times I really don't know my next move. I have made choices in my past I am not proud of, yet you graciously shower on me your love! I do not have to be perfect at all, I simply must know on who to call. In knowing this I have so much power, Even in the darkest of hours. Therefore, I live thankful for your love, knowing nothing   and no one is above! You loved me then, you love me now, this is why my life I vow!

°•o◯o•° ... °•o◯o•° ... °•o◯o•°

Keep Your Eyes On Jesus

When you do not understand, just know God has the plan. If you focus on Jesus, He gives you the map, The keys and the peace, The grace and relief.

He comforts us different than simple man can, He guides, and he shines all holding our hands. Just trust in his ways, even when you have to say, that you know that you know O you know he made the way!

He sends angels to bring, his mighty plan sovereign. So never sweat, don't let the enemy see you fret, No, instead, let him know he's dead, and praise through the storms confusing up his head!

He knows his bed and he's just mad, so never forget what sweet Jesus did! Thee victory is in Christ Jesus, we know, and we see, For this cup Runneth over in his joy and his peace.

°•o◯o•° ... °•o◯o•° ... °•o◯o•°

One Touch

I never walk this road alone, Although, at times, I long for home. Here in this world for now I stay, Lord Jesus Father God have your way! How very thankful I am for your son, He died for me to know your love.

This world it hurts, at times too much, and then you save me with a simple touch! When I cry out O Lord you hear me, I must know it when I just don't see! I want my soul to bless just you, I am constantly asking, what should I do?

O Lord I am hurting, touch my heart, anoint it with your blood and leave your mark. I can't go on without you near, Left or right both choices I fear. When you're here all is well with my soul. Your love I feel it, you let me know. It reaches down to the hurt deep inside, It pulls it out and tears I cry.

You are always my alibi, my everything, you are always right there to rescue me. So, when I hurt, and things seem sad, I see your face and I don't feel so bad! I thank you Lord, I truly do, please show me what you want me to do.

°•o(j)o•°   ...   °•o(j)o•°   ...   °•o(j)o•°

Intercession

What do I do if I should see, discern who it is looking back at me? Yet, what I see is not ripe or light, I see darkness currently winning the fight. I could just choose to walk away, saving my prayers for another day.

My flesh is torn, my heart is burdened, I love so much the one Satan is hurting! He does it often, just as much as he can, his whole life's work is the downfall of man! Since we know just whom we battle with, we must come prepared to withstand him!

Our prayers are heard, our good Father knows, the ways in which the enemy shall go. Sometimes, we just cannot see God saves us painfully from catastrophe! When we see despair, pain, and hurt God and the angels are on operation overt!

It is hard, but we can count it all joy, with our emotions Father will never toy! It may look bad, terrible, or awful yet God has double blessings for our sorrows! See, it's not just something to say "Don't walk by sight, no! Walk by faith!"

Each time we choose in faith to move our prayers break chains of oppression loose! We may not yet see the victory, but we know that we win in the end the enemy is history! Our hearts may be broken, our own dreams seemed crushed, yet he's making beauty out of dust!

When we see a loved one suffer warfare it's important to pray for them and quietly be there. When you pray they don't have to know. God loves to see that to him first we go. He is always responding to our prayers even at times we don't feel like he's there. So many details to us are incomprehensible but we know the life God gives us is truly commendable.

Just imagine greater miracles from you and me, our works are to be beyond what Jesus did. I don't know about you but imagining that is hard for me to do! I cannot imagine greater miracles in you or in me, but then God reminds me of my own story!

Where I know for sure Jesus walked with me, then I sit in awe of his love for me! Ponder the word, where each saint's story is blurred. Their stories seem to come together as one, as they all were accompanied by God's only son. We know this without a doubt at all, for he came just as we each were about to fall.

In our weakness he is strong carrying us, we may never have seen this without any struggles! We know it now so we cannot turn around, we must keep going another round! Yes, we may be bruised, we may be beaten, but we know with sweet Jesus we are never defeated!

So, get down, sit down, however you do; pray in all things that you go through! Pray when you wake up, pray at night, you must pray when it's spiritual warfare you fight! Don't waste your time or energy thinking of what you believe should be!

Go with the flow being sure our God knows every detail and every way to go. God also knows where not to be; he gives us signs, signals and warnings. We often don't see or don't obey then end up hurt and feeling betrayed. This is where we must not stray, we must pray fervently even on good days!

In good times or bad be very thankful, being someone else's guardian angel! Remember in sorrow how Jesus still lived, a lifetime of love he chose to give! If a man of flesh can live without sin, even when we consider all the sorrow he was in; How can we say we can't do something when we have his precious holy spirit within?

How can we become like Jesus? It seems unreachable yet with the holy spirit it is feasible! Believable, achievable, we are redeemable, but we have to know to most people it's inconceivable! We get excited, it's hard to hide it, the love we have for Jesus makes us submit!

He fills us up with hope each time we call his name, he hears our righteous prayers all the same! We have to know when sight doesn't show, our good Father has it under control! Then, when we pray, in faith we say, and mountains will be moved, that's our testimony!

Continue then, loving others strong with unconditional love we can never go wrong! It could never be wasted or go void, just show some love don't be paranoid! The people who hurt you are hurting too otherwise they wouldn't have hurt you! The enemy comes to devour whom he will, he hunts, he plots, and ultimately kills!

We must be steadfast and alert, we cannot be so easily disturbed interceding for all those we know. We must stay calm, we must be steady, in prayer we go, we are always ready! Interceding for all those we, we know it is Father God's favor to be shown! We pray as we say and we do it in   faith for we know Daddy hears us so we smile, love, and wait!

°•○ⓘ○•°   ...   °•○ⓘ○•°   ...   °•○ⓘ○•°

Reflections

When we're hurting again, as we often are, Jesus walks beside us, he is never very far. Often, we feel so alone we cannot bear, yet in the plunging of the heart we must know he is there! This life, this world, are cold and hard, we still must give others the love in our hearts. To give and to love is life's greatest treasure; The world only offers what looks to be better!

When you do something small and someone smiles, that tiny action might travel for miles. They smile all the way to their house, They smile at their children and even their spouse. They talk on the phone to a friend far away, they cheer their family up with love and brighten their day. This tiny action sure went a long way, this all happening in a fraction of a day!

Meanwhile, you smile, as you know you are blessed. You don't have to worry, you don't have to stress. God knows what he's doing, he always knows best! At times it seems hard, we have travelled so far, yet where we are going is worth all the scars! See, people are hurting, heartbroken, even cold; Only the blood of Jesus can heal their souls!

We poke, and prod, get angry and mad, we want them to see what they do is bad. We argue and fight with the people we love, we curse, and we yell, even push and shove. Have we forgotten who it is we fight? Not flesh and blood but evil in the night. The darkness we see, in you and in me, Is always the works of the enemy!

He plots to hurt us and leave us defeated, But Jesus came to give us complete freedom! What a love unexplainable by flesh, He went through hell just to give sinners the best! He was very forgiving, he never sinned, He suffered and endured so we could win! He never thought twice, he just offered his life, to save this world in all its strife!

For you, for me, he died for all, you will always know his signature call. He comes in love, he comes in peace, Through hurt and pain, even physical grief. He never condemns or throws out shade, He simply loves knowing all God made. Sure, people hurt Jesus, we know they did, but he was not an average kid!

He stood apart from the crowd, He spoke so soft yet sounded so loud! People were so drawn to him wanting to be near, He cast away all doubt, confusion and fear! He came with the power of forgiveness and love, Power from nowhere but Heaven above! He came to show us what grace really is, He loved, and he suffered yet he never sinned!

Jesus knew his destiny was simply to win, Win the war against Satan, letting grace in. He had to be the perfect man of flesh, to beat Satan, hell, sin, and death! He came in forgiveness and unconditional love; How God loves the world and gave us his son! If he could ask of us one simple thing, it would be to see himself in you and me!

°•○◌○•° ... °•○◌○•° ... °•○◌○•°

Green And Red Crimson To White

Can you imagine it, being in that boat? You would certainly have to be full of the Holy Ghost! To do as Peter did, not as most, to walk on water, stepping right

84

out of the boat! To trust in Jesus so real and true! I know following him is all I want to do! I have tried this world's many sins, all it did was leave me empty within!

When you have drank from his endless well, nothing in this world can satisfy or fill! At the moment you are tired of your own ways, Sweet Jesus comes rushing in to leave you amazed! We see suddenly he is all, when we choose him, we cannot fall! If we fall, it is not a failure, it is simply the will of God's divine nature.

This type of faith requires constant renewal, for we know how the enemy seeks to kill and to ruin! If you watch for the thief, you will see, He can work through you and through me! We therefore must choose to be renewed, in all we say and all we do! Do not be so quick to get angry and react, Instead, see Jesus behavior in the past!

He was regularly mistreated and abused, Yet, to react is something he did not choose. He had a goal from the very start, He turned to Father to ease his heart. Only our Father can do this right, we look by day, we search by night. We must fix our eyes upon the cross, just look to see all Jesus lost!

He did not do a bit of it for himself, No, quite opposite, he did it for everybody else! To know that truth, deep in your soul, makes you realize who it is that makes you whole! We have much to give in this life, we must know to suffer is to be like Christ! We must push on, rain or shine!

I know I will for Jesus is mine! To have, to hold, I do wed thee forever and ever in holy matrimony! And, if one day God sends me a husband, Jesus will be that third cord of strength and love!

They say call out onto the Lord, He will turn into beauty what once was discord. I tried it all, surely every stone overturned, I see now that it was lessons I had to learn. One thing I know to be complete truth, if you call on Jesus, he will save you!

At times, you may not see his hand. His ways are beyond what we understand. Other times you feel that sweet and genuine comfort, those blessings of peace and hope come forth. You know with all your heart and being, He rescued you when your heart was bleeding. You know very well how broken you are, so how else do you walk like you have no scars?

You feel the pain amid the rain, you know that only he takes it all away! You call on him, tears pouring down, He makes a smile from what was a frown. This strength is not of me, not my own, yet he wants me to let it be shown.

In love he comes to make a way, where you wouldn't have made it another day. When this grace meets you where you are, it awakens your senses; your heart is jarred. You look around and see things new, He found his place right inside of you!

°•o◌o•° ... °•o◌o•° ... °•o◌o•°

His Way

God has the plan, I'm just a man. Living in this world, completely misunderstood. I mind my own business, I keep to myself; I wish I could say the same for everyone else. I feel things, I see things, nobody understands, Yet I am the one to lend a helping hand. I know that it is worth it to help and to care, but sometimes I need for someone to be there.

To be my crutch when I've had enough, A physical hug; is that asking too much? I don't think so, but most people do. I wonder could they walk a day in my shoes? To feel what I feel and think what I think, most people couldn't make it, in sorrow they'd shrink.

Yet people aren't the ones who will truly support you, God gives comfort to his truly anointed. So, life goes on, along with the struggle, piece by piece God reveals the puzzle! People and things, they come and go, God's love for us is a constant glow! I look to the left and to the right, I see him there even on the darkest nights! I hope no one goes through what I have yet the truth is they do and it's very sad! No matter what, remember this one thing, in God's love we have all to gain!

°•○◌○•°   ...   °•○◌○•°   ...   °•○◌○•°

Yes Lord

Yes, Jesus I do believe I said yes! It was not just yesterday your spirit I kissed! No, it goes way back far it goes, back to things evil wants me not to know! Certainly, Father always had his hand upon everything I ever touched my heart on!

People never liked me genuinely, Father keep me focused they see Jesus, not me! At painful moments I can forget; Truly it was only for love I submit! To years of tears and painful fears only wanting love to be near! Ghosts and monsters all around, how could it feel like a playground?

Yet I see it was never meant to be one, My life was never set out to be fun! My entire life was one huge lesson of what searching for love the messes we get in! All of it was your plan Lord, you planned it all out just for your glory! So, your precious love others would see, for if you can love me you can love anybody!

They call me every name under the son yet never see that all loving one! I cannot allow deception any longer, God does not want hate to ponder! And sweet Jesus he cries for you, He cries constantly for your soul too! Can't you see his love so real? Just call on his name, he will show himself true!

°•○◍○•°   ...   °•○◍○•°   ...   °•○◍○•°

The Joy Of The Lord Is My Strength

As I sit here in complete awe of you Lord, I realize we live glory to glory. We come, and we go doing what you want, we will suffer much to live this beautiful plot. I always end up right back at the cross, to die is gain, in Christ is no loss! In moments of struggle, of pain or not knowing, you always come through and show love to me.

We must realize and truly see this life is but a vapor, we live for eternity! We must be thankful no matter what because we know our creator is an awesome God! He knows the end from the beginning, one day at a time we are winning! At times, it does not feel that way, in fact it can feel quite opposite.

Yet, we remain strong in the faith, reading your living word every day. Some days we will read it all day just to be able to keep our strength. Why? Because every promise is real and reading it repeatedly helps it sink in! Thank you, Lord, for a reason to live, serving with love, giving all I can give.

It truly is all for you Jesus, after all, look what you've done for us! There is so much joy in serving the Lord, whether others receive it or are appreciative. In the end, it's not about them, it's only about whether we truly listened.

Did we do as Father God said, whether our love was accepted or rejected? When our love is truly genuine, they don't reject us, they reject Father God. Listening to Daddy is everything, no matter how much we are struggling. From glory to glory the just live by faith, and true faith says God already made a way!

°•o(j)o•°   ...   °•o(j)o•°   ...   °•o(j)o•°

The Helper

It is amazing what a day can do, God always makes me feel brand new! I feel so strong but it's not me, for sweet Jesus is constantly interceding! I will give credit right where it's due, in this life I want to be true!

I've never felt the need to lie, I often wonder how people do it and why? It's sad to say they are not content, with their own life so the truth they bend. It does not matter what others think, it only matters what God sees.

I know that I have seen a lot, not just bad, although that was the enemy's plot. The happy memories do survive. Through pain and struggle I am alive! There is one thing I long to do; To help other people not feel so blue.

God knowing my deepest desires, I suppose therefore I go through the fire! One thing I know for certain, how can I help others if I've never had burdens? When someone needs specific help, you must have gone through it yourself.

I would not expect understanding, unless you also have had crash landings. My life could be a bestselling book, about what the enemy stole and took. But more and more my heart is right where it is supposed to be, So I can help others to the truth to be set free!

I know it might sound totally crazy, but my life overall is truly amazing! From the outside looking in, you may wonder how I feel I win? Yes, in my life I've had many trials, Many things I went through and could not smile!

At times, I sat, I cried, and wondered; Why me Lord? Why storms and thunder? But God is faithful and loves our souls, He takes and gives wanting nothing above him! One thing is still so very true, He only wants what's best for you!

When we see it simply this way, even on the worst of days, we can have faith and truly believe, his children he will never leave! He needs people to work for him; To be honest enough to look within!

That is where he placed our future, it has been there since our birth. I don't think God could be any prouder, when we give our love louder and louder! I hope that I can help this lost world, Doing so one by one, boy and girl.

I feel this is what he wants from me, too many people are not set free! So, I push on, the show must go; At times it's hard but you may never know. I want to help the world to see, they can pray and be set free!

°•°o⊙o•° ... °•°o⊙o•° ... °•°o⊙o•°

The Key

Truth is righteousness, don't let the enemy mess with your head! He just knows he is already dead, when you get that faith anything you can tread, clearly you can see, not what's in your head, But, what is destiny! There is only one route; Nothing else shall ever do!

He is sweet king Jesus, that is who, how, and the great why, So, seek him out, on eagle wings he flies! He sees every little tiny disguise, with eyes of faith, yes, spiritual eyes but first you must have ears, Spiritual ears so that you can hear! Just what it is that is destiny, just what is meant for eternity! So, I just dare you to say the name of our king, then you will begin this sweet journey, Only Jesus has your key...

°•○◍○•° ... °•○◍○•° ... °•○◍○•°

The Gospel Truth

Truly I say this pain paved the way. In his arms joy came through this rain. It is not pleasant nor comfortable, yet required in order that we may grow. See the things we need to see, Place all things at sweet Jesus feet!

At times we try so hard, yet we fall, because truly trying is laying down all. In our weakest most painful moments, Father God shines his love on us. In a moment when you are on your knees, it truly hurts yet Father it pleases!

The mighty one who created it all, the one thing he wants is on him shall we call. Just rest just rest oh surely, I say, Father God always makes a way out of no way. See, the way I make always ends in shame, guilt and rejection they know my name!

O but I know Jesus and he saved me! He died on the cross for God's glory! As I am looking back with a vision of discerning, I see Jesus was always right here with me! As a young child so scared and afraid, To this very crazy and beautiful day!

Surely, he suffered on this Earth, all to prove Father's love and your worth! He came out of love for the body of us, He came, and he suffered enduring death on the cross! As hard as it is my brothers and sisters, we have to do it, look what sweet Jesus did!

Surely eyes nor ears they do not know, the ways of which our Father goes. Yet he knows O how he knows, in despair grace and mercy, he shows! He loves me, he loves you, it is true! He died yet he lives in you!

Because the enemy was defeated! Because death Satan fell short in completing! Lord Jesus sits at the right hand of God, constantly interceding for all of us! Sweet Jesus Lord Jesus Father God, When I think about your sweet love!

My heart melts; my pain is gone, once again in death I have won! I thank you Jesus! I thank you Daddy! I could never go back to before you had me! It is well even in worldly hell, For the enemy defeated evil man shall fail!

The sword is sharp, it is double edged; It cuts like a razor right at the head! It hurts it wounds for only you see, as we seek you it is victory! Taking captive every thought and imagination, to think as you would and do as you do!

°•o◖•° ... °•o◖•° ... °•o◖•°

His Throne

Just when you think God has done enough, He showers down some more of his love! He pours it, so you know it's him, He lets us know through him we win! He does not care if we are perfect, He knows that we could never deserve it! Yet, we are faithful day and night, when he says go, we stand and fight! When he says stay, we stand still, knowing his moves, he will reveal! One by one and piece by piece, He gives new love just when we need! See, we must always choose him first. Nothing or no one can have more worth! Then his love will truly work, No matter what relationship we nurture! I am sure of one thing alone, God almighty sits on his throne!

°•○◯○•° ... °•○◯○•° ... °•○◯○•°

Real Life Real Love

I feel so different than I once did! I almost feel like I was a thirty-year-old kid! And, in many was I was! Thank God I see and know what love in action does! Miracles, wonders, and magical hours; This is what our Daddy showers!

He showers you, he showers me, like him is all I want to be! Looking back, the road was long, when I think of why I stop and pause. Now, it is easier since I have a cause, yes, you Jesus are my purpose! You are the way! What a refreshing start of the day! To live for you is so much better than when I had storms alone to weather!

I always felt alone, although I never was. I just had to see you surrounded me with love! I once was blind with no help, thinking only of myself! Now, since I come last, real life real love has come to pass! This is not by my works or ways, it is only by the precious blood of Jesus!

°•○◯○•° ... °•○◯○•° ... °•○◯○•°

Glory Glory Hallelujah

Oh, my goodness your glory your glory! Your hand has certainly touched all my story! I look to the times when I was lost, when I was so hurt and felt so past gone. I realize now how you were carrying me. I know that strength was beyond what I can be.

At those moments looking back, I really stood tall like I knew you were all that. Yet, at those times I did not know, my love for you had yet to grow. Now I know back I could never go, I only want for your love to show!

Show your love through me each day, in all I do, in every way! All I ask Oh Lord of you, is that in me your will, you do. I give in, I totally give up, the only thing that satisfies me is your love! Therefore, I know your way is right, I look by day and am still at night.

°•o⊙o•° ... °•o⊙o•° ... °•o⊙o•°

Sovereign

It is so easy in this life to get overwhelmed, one thing after another the enemy sends. Then I realize I am in your hands, there is nothing that can change your plan! I listened when it just didn't make sense, So, I have faith you are bringing me out of this!

So many things I could worry about, Yet I know too well there is no time for doubt. One day at a time I must do as you say, I believe you, Abba, will make a way. In my human mind I reason with logic, I must remember all the power you got it.

You Daddy hold the world in your hands, Your ways are beyond what I understand. I cannot afford to waiver left or right, The enemy only wants to ignite fright!

Then, feeling overwhelmed within, I don't even want tomorrow to begin. See, the evil one is so strategic, He comes in like a flood again and again. Faith in God is so powerful, Otherwise, what we see makes us unsure!

°•○◎○•° ... °•○◎○•° ... °•○◎○•°

Free Will

God help us all, Lord knows we need it. Babies having babies and they can't even feed them. People dying over nothing at all, and no one seems to take the fall. Grandparents so sweet and dear, People act as though they are not even here. Just living for the moment, not caring for others, When in God's eyes we're all sisters and brothers.

I myself am sick and tired! Our entire world needs to be re- wired! I can sit and wonder who can, Or I can get up and lend a helping hand! It starts with love and tender care, it's easy to show and share! I know in the past your heart has been hurt, But God knew you needed hard times to learn.

He wants you to love your sisters and brothers, it shouldn't be hard to love one another! There are many people lost, scared, and alone; Nobody to call when they pick up the phone! A smile, a few words, can go a long way; You might help someone make it one more day!

See, you never know what one person has suffered. If only we could think about one another! It's not a risk, you have been hurt before! God is always there when you knock on his door! So, do me a favor, I dare you to try, or you can just sit there and die on the inside! It's your choice and your life, but it feels so good to do something right!

At the end of the day we all need love, we can all show others the love we get from God! I myself have been hurt most of my life, Yet I choose to love because I know it is right! I want you to try, I am begging you, after all, what do you really have to lose?

°•₀ₒ₀ₒ•° ... °•₀ₒ₀ₒ•° ... °•₀ₒ₀ₒ•°

Repent! The Kingdom of God is At Hand!

Thee greatest feeling in life is seeing the power of God's love heals those around us! When you realize his love for you, it awakens love for all people! Everyone's heart cries out to Jesus, it is just many people cannot see this! We all have years of fears and tears, but it fades away knowing Jesus is near!

That lie, that fear, is just a snare! Death, destruction, hurting; this is how the enemy resides within! See, God knew all your sins, past and future, the day he created you! Repent and believe in sweet Jesus for God sent us his only begotten son! He does not love you or me any less than he loves Christ Jesus!

97

His only son came from heaven to hell to save us all and every knee shall bow! What do you stress about or long for? Truly only in Jesus you will find the cure! In finding Jesus, we are cured to be the cure; the cure of the sickness of the world! Only the blood of Jesus can save us, first you must believe he is God's son and died for us! Come as you are, God loves you, while we were yet sinners Christ died for you too!

°•○◎○•° ... °•○◎○•° ... °•○◎○•°

Free

Father, I know what you told me, I have felt your touch, yet everything I am seeing is quite opposite. I must still trust, keep marching on, even if I am not sure exactly what's going on. I pray for guidance, for your will, yet it seems you are telling me just be still.

Yet, I also hear "I am perfecting your will, I am ensuring your life is in my will. "When I don't understand, I just pray to God because nobody can help me the way he can. I must live like I am loved because really and truly I am deeply loved! No more hopelessness, even in chains, no matter what his love remains!

I know you are uncomfortable baby, trust me I know, in time you will see how much you have grown! I know you want answers, I know you need guidance, trust and believe I am allowing you to find them! Remember, faith is in what we don't yet see, the things Father God is promising.

See, Father God is very jealous, he cannot stand anything or anyone above his love. I asked for him to make my heart secure, then I instantly wondered what I was asking for.

Lord I need you always and forever, I don't know what's next but you're there and I remember. Without you Jesus no doubt I'd be done, I must remember you have already won!

It is difficult when all odds are against me, yet if God is for me it is all sovereign! O Lord please guide me every day, I feel your breakthrough is on the way! I receive all you want for me in Jesus name, I don't even know what it is I claim! Wow! Yes! That is faith, and faith far beyond what I can understand! I can do all things through Christ who strengthens me, I need your power of love to set me totally free!

°•○◌○•° ... °•○◌○•° ... °•○◌○•°

Divine Order

Sometimes, in my mind, I wonder off; I sit and ponder all your costs! I add them up, it equals loss! I do not know how you paid them all! The fact is still the very same, there is power at the mention of your name!

Just study his life, Jesus is strength, He suffered so much yet was without sin! In your suffering you are like him, it makes it easier your love to give! He gave and gave and gave some more, just so we could enter Heaven's door!

You see, in his death we are forgiven, for all our sins we ever committed! Love one, love all, this is why, for you and me sweet Jesus died! But, of course, death could never hold him! It's in this hope we stand on a whim.

On that whim, we can stand firm; Nothing shall prosper against us it all shall burn! Ashes Ashes everywhere, what will you do? Does your heart care? My heart cares, it always has, on your worst days it is not that bad!

You must stop thinking of you and only you, and think about what Christ Jesus would do! When carrying out this divine order, your love can have no single border! No boundaries, that's not how Jesus worked!

If you must question it just go back on his word! You see, it's love, that's what it is! Love's where it starts and where it ends! It sounds so easy but where do we begin? I have been asking myself this very question.

I then look at my life in the form of lessons, I realize the pain and suffering was in disguise a blessing! I am filled with joy my life was full of trials and struggles, to be like you Jesus is worth the suffering!

I will never give up on God, hope, peace, and love; A divine order from Heaven above! His presence, his grace makes it so easy, in those moments' life is so pleasing! So, find that place and stay right there, for I'd rather be not anywhere else!

°•o⊕o•° ... °•o⊕o•° ... °•o⊕o•°

Jesus! Jesus!

I call on you, in all I have and all I do! For this reason, all your power is mine, you give it to me and it is divine! Divine order, it is simply so! You come and go until you know! But, once you know, there is no return, No one could tell you what you're not worth! You are a precious gift of love, you have much worth in God above! You have had this precious worth, Even before the moment of your birth!

°•°o(o)o•° ... °•°o(o)o•° ... °•°o(o)o•°

Faith, Hope, and Love

This life can be so hard, no doubt about that, we must stand strong knowing we are hard pressed! To live to Jesus is to die to self, and every moment we need his power and help. From glory to glory is our testimony, the enemy only wants our joy and peace.

We cannot go by what is seen for we have great hope in heavenly things. There's never been such a time as this, the world is lost and only in Jesus do we win. Faith is priceless, it's all we have, even when everything might look bad. We know God knows every detail, if we just trust him we will not derail.

We may fall but we get back up, all because of God's only begotten son. God has an undying love for us, his promise stands good no matter what. He never said it would be without struggle, he did say trust him to get us through! Things happen, this world is so cold, no doubt their hearts have been waxed over.

We must continue to love the least of us even when it seems like it is just too much. Even when we may want to give up, we remember sweet Jesus never gave up on us! He humbled himself to death on a cross, he suffered so much more than we ever could!

He put himself completely to the side, so ultimately the devil he could smite! He shed his blood, his precious blood, for sinners like us to be forgiven! When we focus on the victory in that, we see there is no turning back! We must press on to the kingdom of Heaven, we must continue to sharpen our weapons! We must know the kingdom of heaven suffers violence, casting down every imagination, our weapons not carnal! Pray fervently all day every day, do what you can do God already made a way! So often it is just beyond our vision, he is always teaching us for Christ's mission! Continue in hope have faith and know God loves me and he loves you too!

°•○ⓜ○•° ... °•○ⓜ○•° ... °•○ⓜ○•°

Prodigal Children

The prodigal children are coming; don't fret. Although, for now, they are the living dead. You can help, pray with intercession. Favor then pours down from Heaven.

I see your tears, I know your pain; Yet still grace, hope, and love remain. I want you near, I try to tell you. Yet you are more interested in what to do. Sometimes you don't have to do a thing, just sit back and know I am sovereign. I fight your battles and victory is mine, So, go ahead and shine, just shine!

102

The time you live on earth can be divine, but only when you choose to shine. Trouble will come, but it also will go, in this we trust; deep down we know! Don't stress, don't worry, it is in his hands, not a thing can ever be done by man. You must know my way prevails, don't you remember my hands were nailed? I came and suffered for you, don't you see? I came so that you would have life everlasting!

°•○○○•° ... °•○○○•° ... °•○○○•°

Romans 8:28

A piece of history, with me personally, I sinned so much just wanting to be loved. Then, I found God's love, only through Jesus. I began to see the power of Jesus, the love he had for me no matter what I did. I shed my deathly fleshly self, it was not easy, but Jesus was my help. He keeps on asking, even in small things, I just keep listening as he mounts me on eagle wings.

Listen to the tiny little whispers of love from above, and be amazed when you choose God's love! I have seen some of God's biggest dreams come true, just because in him I choose. See, it is not always huge, the smallest things Father God he uses. So, listen and do not be afraid, because his ways for us simply amaze! Family first, this is his word, Rest assured you are completely covered!

The very thing he wants for you, just may require you first to lose. Father has a perfect plan, Romans 8:28 for every woman and man. Might I ask you to remember, how life was for Christ our savior. Suffering o yes unlike another, So, trust in this, you can recover!

Suffering for you and me, really truly is God's glory! For me, I choose in Jesus to lose, anything he cannot use. Surely, yes, there is much suffering, which for many years came fiercely to me. Now, I still suffer at the hands of others, But, the great difference is in armor I am covered.

°•○①○•° ... °•○①○•° ... °•○①○•°

Hypocrites

Sometimes in life I just don't know what to do which way to go. I feel so helpless at this point in time, yet I know I am not God's got my life! Being in the wilderness it is for him, I must remember in the end we win!

Truly it is not about what I want, it is not about anything except Father God! The beautiful thing about God's glory is deep down that's what satisfies me! To see one person, have some hope makes every sacrifice and obedience worth it!

So many, too many, religious hypocrites, who truly don't know what real love is! They want to judge and condemn people claiming God yet being evil! The time is now for them to repent, Father God is not having it! All through the Bible we see God is love, why do so many not love the least of us?

Why do people walk around and condemn not knowing or caring where someone else has been? Truly, this grieves Father God's heart, and Jesus will say workers of iniquity departs! If Jesus died for forgiveness and love, who at all could say they are above?

Who would dare to think they are above anyone else when Jesus died for sinners not the self-righteous? People look at others who struggle and start assuming and thinking they know! Really only God does and no matter what he still loves us!

If the church could put away their pride, they could see we are all hurting inside! They might realize only Jesus reigns; they would change the way they do things! Sad but true, in this world selfishness rules, people only bring about their own ruin!

Father God sees everything, he hears our thoughts, he wants our hearts, he wants every part! When we give our will up for him, no matter what we always win! He made us and knows the desires of our heart; from our own ways we must depart!

Will we suffer? What did Jesus do? Just think about it, of course we will! Sweet Jesus suffered his entire life, he didn't turn left, he never looked right! He came to do Father God's will and the religious people ended up killing him! It truly is sad what religion does, it is the opposite of loving the least of us!

We each have a process with Father God, we should not be shunning anyone! Now, pure evil is different and obvious, usually they are the ones doing the sunning of Father's kids! Oppression is real, and it is the enemy, thus if you boast, boast in Christ Jesus! The world is the enemy of the cross, in the end it is truly their loss!

°•○◌○•° ... °•○◌○•° ... °•○◌○•°

Spirit Kills Flesh

I lived my entire life for what I thought was true and right. The problem was I was totally lost, I didn't know Jesus as I do now. But, all my life I suffered divinely, still in painful moments it doesn't seem right.

To love those around you so very much, to know all they need is God's one simple touch. Yet they reach for every other thing, a fake friend, weed, pills, a cigarette, or a drink. It is not about judging them, it is more about souls and loving them!

I have tried it all in this world, yes, this is how I know the real cure! I know the enemy can put us in our own cell, right up in our minds in our own hell! He will use any and everything he can, he has perfected deceit since the fall of man!

He only seeks to kill and destroy; crazy thing is he makes bad look good. Then, of course, he makes good look bad leaving Father's children to be sad. But, this world is perishing, even sorrow and pain is temporary.

In those times we realize just how much we are loved thinking of how much Jesus suffered for us. For God so loved the world that he gave his only begotten son, not for a few or some, for everyone. But, just as in Adam and Eve, we have choices every single being.

The beautiful thing about choosing Jesus, he loved us first and left the Holy Spirit. Piece by piece we are made new, but only if we should so choose. Then, this life has purpose, otherwise our soul we lose, and life is worthless!

°•○◯○•° ... °•○◯○•° ... °•○◯○•°

Forgiven

Can you imagine God's perfect plan? He has one for every woman and every man! Surely glory flows higher through my veins if only each soul would give Father the reins. Not Luke warm or even hot, With Jesus Christ fire is what we got!

Looking back, it was very difficult, yet now I see God is always on the move. Now don't get it wrong I'm not trying to Twist it, if you don't see my suffering, then the point you missed it. I cried many tears, years upon years, to be where

I am today right here. It was not pretty, it was not fair, God wanted me to see mercy and grace are everywhere. Many days I sinned and also nights, Only the blood of Jesus makes it brand new and right. I looked everywhere in everything, yes high and low I searched for me!

I had to see in Jesus is my identity, my very being Jesus, our eternity. Now, an entire lifetime of hurt and pain falls on my face like drops of rain. Yet it seems that joy reigns, only because of sweet Jesus very being!

Many years I suffered without knowing him, Now I surrender, my life I shall give! Many people are lost and deceived yet I know the cure, it is the best-selling book in the whole wide world! Open it up and read, the heart begins pure, a journey with Jesus yes glory for sure!

✿°•○◎○•°✿ ... ✿°•○◎○•°✿ ... ✿°•○◎○•°✿

His Name

what is this love I stumbled upon, I found it when I was on the run! I lost my way oh so long ago, yet through it all your love still shows. Your hand was there all along, including the times when I was wrong. Oh Lord Jesus thank you is too simple, I live my life to be your example.

Do as you wish Father, as you will, I must be sure all my flesh I kill. Daily, yes daily, surely all day, I call on your name to lead the way. The crazy beautiful you always amaze, the sorrow and hurts it's not truly pain. The joy and the strength come from rain, truly to suffer is in Christ to gain!

All this joy it once was pain, it all began to change on one day. A day I began to have faith in a name, a name above all names, puts them all to shame! But, more than a name, sweet Jesus you reign; you rescued me and became my king!

I don't even deserve this love you give, yet every day you continue to give it. You are right here in front of me, on the North, South, West, and the East. I truly could never thank you enough, I must live to share in this love.

It is free to all and so priceless, the proof is there on Jesus wrists! So, don't you think for one single second, for any reason this love you can't get. He died for you all the same, if you don't believe me just call his sweet name!

°•o(ɔ)o•°   ...   °•o(ɔ)o•°   ...   °•o(ɔ)o•°

No Fear

People shall say how dare you smile? How dare you think you are forgiven by God? Just keep on smiling, let them see me, No matter the amount of animosity. Do you hear me and are you listening? Everything is simply Ephesians.

Warrior go warrior girl, you are destined to rock this world. You, my love, my sweet beloved, they got to see you, the true struggle. No more living in a bubble of trouble, you know my protection goes unimaginable. Your shield, you need it, don't forget. Oh yes and your breastplate of righteousness.

Also, your belt of truth, and make sure you have the salvation helmet on you! Always remember that peace and grace in those shoes, you will need them to spread this great news! Above all your sword must be sharp, it will be the light piercing the darkness. Now, you see, the battle is near, but don't you ever fear, sweet Jesus is here.

°•o(ɔ)o•°   ...   °•o(ɔ)o•°   ...   °•o(ɔ)o•°

Ignorant Bliss

Looking back, I stand in awe, every mistake was a part of God's will. How does this work, it seems impossible, he took all my grief and made it beautiful! He loved me long before I was ever born, long before my heart was ever torn. This love, yes, that's what it is, I just want someone else to experience this!

I spent so many years trying to find what or who would fill the void inside. Now I see, I realize, God made the hole so him we would find. Sadly, we get hurt in the meantime, looking to the world to satisfy. No money, nobody, no place or substance compares to the love that Jesus has for us!

Each time we choose anything but him we will be left feeling empty within. Yet, Oh how beautiful if we choose, it is peace beyond understanding knowing Jesus! To be known, inside and out, and to be radically loved without a doubt! Isn't that what we're searching for? Nothing else is enough, we're always wanting more.

Yet, Oh how opposite it is loving Jesus, we may have nothing yet have everything in him. It's a feeling and I cannot explain it, it's a fire and I cannot contain it! Looking back and seeing myself looking for worth in everything else. Now I see my true identity, it's not in a job, education, or money.

Who I am rests firmly in God, the world is deceived and totally lost. It truly is deception and the enemy plots; the world needs to see this and get back to God! For in God's wisdom they deny him, using science, math, or whatever they can. It breaks my heart, it's come to this, so many living in ignorant bliss.

°•○ⓘ○•° ... °•○ⓘ○•° ... °•○ⓘ○•°

Gossip

When we think we know someone, only from something that someone else said, we do ourselves and them an injustice. See, God created each one of us, Father God loves all his children. Truth be told he even loved the devil, So, who are we to walk around and judge?

Who are we to assume anything? Jesus loves us, yes everybody! He died for the world while it was sinning, He knew that through his blood we were winning! They talked so terribly bad about sweet Jesus, I am sure it hurt him yet Satan he defeated! Can you imagine most people hating you?

Yet, you just loved them knowing the plan God had for you! Not only this, but dying for them, as they blasphemed your name and called you a sinner! Looking back, word of Christ Jesus spread fast, People seem to degrade what they don't understand. Think about it, Jesus had no sin, which means he only had love within.

He healed the sick, gave sight to the blind, yet everyone thought he was out of his mind! He was real, he was honest, he just loved; Yet they looked down on Jesus like they were above! We cannot go around judging everyone, When Christ Jesus greatest commandment is love! We may not understand someone else, But, let us remember Father God does!

Too often we as humans go off someone's past, Yet, sweet Christ Jesus died for forgiveness! This means we should look at today's fruits, Not last week and certainly not years ago! We know with God anything is possible, in loving someone genuinely, it gives them room to grow!

The moment we open our mouths and speak negative, Is the very same moment we allow Satan in! We all have been, or are guilty of it, But, let us refrain from anything negative! See, when we ask God to forgive us with a contrite heart, He forgets everything we've done, we have a brand-new start!

°•○⊙○•° ... °•○⊙○•° ... °•○⊙○•°

No Time To Play

God is edifying the body of Christ, get in where you belong or get left behind! It sounds so harsh, so down right wrong, Yet, God is saying he has given us so long! The time has come, it is now and done, there is no turning back and you cannot run!

Pleasure seekers, secret sinners your time has come, He waits for each of us in all of our undone. He loves us all, he wants us each home with him, but as much as you take are you willing to give? And, as much as you give are you willing to take? In doing God's will you shall encounter heart break.

This is the anointing, it is not you; You have always known in all you do. Now, you can say "I am redeemed", For who the Son sets free is free indeed! Unity! Unity! Unity! I hear Father roar, As if in the ring with a bull and matador. His nostrils are flaring, steaming non-stop, our fleshly ways and meager lives we must drop!

Submit to Father, he is zealous for you, with him by your side there's nothing you cannot do! Just know with your very being, there is only one way to God you see! His name is known throughout eternity; He gave his life for you and for me! It is the sweetest name we could ever speak, The name above all names, the name of Christ Jesus!

I promise his will for your life is right, the enemy is prowling like a thief at night. Submit to Father, do not turn away, every day you will be simply amazed. So today I say tomorrow is new, For surely Christ Jesus rests within you.

°•o(ŋ)o•°   ...   °•o(ŋ)o•°   ...   °•o(ŋ)o•°

Identity

Telling of the goodness of Jesus, answering question after question. I acknowledge more of your glory, how you redeemed my story. You broke me to pieces, brought me down to my knees, you made me see only you Jesus! I am not who I once was, every day I find myself, I find me as I find more of you Lord.

I struggle when I have all I need, you live right here inside of me! I just could never understand why you chose me, such a wretched human. You love me more than I can comprehend, O without you I am just a wretched woman! You came into my life, you washed me clean and white. You made every wrong right, you hold me tight every night!

What else can I say, I love you, you are my greatest love story! You took my sins away and made it all for your glory! It is so obvious when you re-write stories! You give peace, hope, and joy while taking worries! You are simply beautiful beyond amazing! No matter what happens you amaze me!

Truth is, I lost my life, the life I live, I live to Christ! But O to die is truly gain, for now, your sweet spirit reigns! O how I am changed, I could never be the same! You took my heart of stone and gave me a heart of flesh, you gave me beauty for my ashes! I only want to do as you say, sometimes myself gets in the way!

I only steal my own joy and peace trying to Do things my own way. Your will your way, listening to what you say, this brings peace and joy to my day! I realize just how much you love me, and whom the son sets free is free indeed! I only want for the hurting and lost to see just how much this world costs! To see what they gain when themselves they lose, to see the benefit of gaining you!

Suffering, yes it does abound, people need to see you can turn it all around! I know the cure for the world, to accept Jesus Christ, he already accepted you! He shed his blood and suffered for us, to be set free and feel that freedom! In a dark and cruel world, I feel free, I feel loved, I feel redeemed! All this Jesus precious blood did for me, there is no greater love than sweet Jesus! I can truly live for once, knowing the deep and wide love you have for me Jesus!

Realizing your death on the cross, it was our gain at your cost! Seeing what you did out of pure love, Just for sinners like us! Let them see you Jesus, let them feel you, I just want souls to know the real you! The one who is honest and still loves, the one who is there no matter what! Let them see you sweet Jesus, O how I know They need you Lord Jesus!

°•o(ı)o•° ... °•o(ı)o•° ... °•o(ı)o•°

Rejected for God's Glory

To be rejected is to be as heaven is, in a tornado of lies everyone says their going. Yet, the truth they don't even want to hear, and it seems me they don't want to be near. So, busy this world seems to be, yet the one who died for them they don't see. So selfish in their day to day lives. Yet, they look down on people as if they're wise.

It is not wise to be asleep right now, look around, Jesus is soon to come on clouds. Yet status and money are so prominent, when none of this will get you into heaven. The world is so lost it breaks God's heart, therefore

the true remnant is on the alter. Being rejected and left for dead, yet inside their heart only love exists.

No time is there to hate or to hurt, we have true assurance in God's holy word. We know that sweet Jesus was rejected, we know he prayed, loved, and dealt with it. He did all that without any sin, to be sure the door to heaven would win. He is the way, the truth, and the life; this world's ways could never be right.

We must know as in the days of Noah, many shall laugh and call us a joke. Sadly, they play with their own souls, to be content and comfortable in the devil's world. We must continue to fight the good fight, when the world does us wrong we still do right. People are not who we live for yet living for God we still want their hearts.

We want them to see who Jesus truly is, a relationship with him, not a religion. We must know we will be hurt, on our names people will throw dirt. We must push on, we must endure, for we have rewards out of this world. If we reach out telling the pure truth, it is not on us what people may choose. I am seeing it is not me they reject, truly, they reject our precious Christ Jesus.

°•o◍o•° ... °•o◍o•° ... °•o◍o•°

This Is Not My Home

Moments in life I long for something...I have Jesus but in Heaven is our home, for now this lonely earth I roam. I realize no matter what, no matter all you give, no matter the joy, there are still moments I long for more, I know it is because this is not our home, if only the world could know.

So many worldly things offered to fill the void, yet none of them can give you true joy! Things and people can bring you happiness, but only sweet Jesus can bring joyful rest. In the middle of a mess we can trust God for in Christ Jesus the battle is won!

Days as today I don't know what it is, maybe it's just my heart longs for my mansion. In the same precious breath, I am so thankful, I have never felt this way before. Completely thankful for life yet ready to go home, my heart says come Lord Jesus come! Yet I also want to live and do God's will, he breathed his life in me O how beautiful!

Now, every day I want to live, everyday his love I want to give. I want to be led by his precious spirit, I want to do as he wants for me. Yet I am also longing to be with God, for truly my home is not this world. I am not of this world, just in it, while God has me here I'm going to make the best of it.

In my opinion there is only one real way to do it, that is to let God's love run fluid. I shine a smile everywhere I go, even if I am not okay myself. Because this world needs to know just how deep and how wide is God's love. How can we expect the world to know unless the love of Jesus we constantly show?

Planting seeds with only one real guarantee, knowing God is pleased with us doing the right thing. Knowing, when we are rejected by man we are still so very loved by him. Knowing, when we are all alone, we are never truly alone with him. Knowing, to listen to him no matter what, this is where real satisfaction comes from. Knowing, in the end when Jesus comes back, we shall here come into my kingdom job well done!

°•o(i)o•°   ...   °•o(i)o•°   ...   °•o(i)o•°

Eternity

That magical and emotional minute as I realize no matter what if I have God I'm winning. All my life I have been rejected, yet, all my life God kept me protected! If God is for me who can be against me? Do I really care what people think? Truth is, they don't

117

even know real love, they claim they do but reject God above.

So many lost and thinking they are alright, it is so sad, my heart cries inside. Jesus was rejected too so I count it an honor to suffer as he did. For if this world loved me chances are God would judge me! I am free, covered by the blood, it no longer matters who rejects my love. I must push on towards the crown, casting all negative imaginations down!

I am here for God's glory, to tell of Jesus is my story! I can't change where I have been, but I am forgiven of all my sins! God alone knows my truth all the way back to my youth. People gossip, hate, or judge yet have no clue of what went on. On the surface it looks one way, truth be told it is quite opposite.

I don't have the time or energy to convince, in the end I stand alone in judgement! And, when that day comes, and I face the son, I look to hear faithful servant job well done! I shall shine before Father as pure gold because when he sees me he sees Jesus low and behold!

Firm I stand on every one of God's promises, all my hope, all my trust I put in him. Therefore, the world can hate me, they can talk about me or debate me. When I am doing what God wants I am happy and satisfied living for God. This world is not my home, I know my home and where I shall go!

Not one single person can stop God, he gives me honest, pure, and perfect love! It pours out of my heart, even to people who might not deserve. That's the point, Jesus died for us all, even the ones nobody loves. He said what we do to the least of us we do onto sweet Jesus himself.

Without loving others no matter what we cannot truly say that we love Father God. So many cannot seem to comprehend, my heart burns for their souls in the long run. I don't care if they hate me, I still don't want anyone in hell for eternity.

°•○⑪○•°   ...   °•○⑪○•°   ...   °•○⑪○•°

Begin Again

My heart is hurting, I don't quite know why, I feel this deep pain and I can't deny. What am I doing, to where will I go? This world, I know, is not my home. I try my best to fight the good fight, I get so sad at times I don't want to try.

I know God has been here all along, but it sure is hard at times to move on. I have been labelled everything but good, for most of my life I have been so misunderstood. I realize now that all the names even I myself began to believe.

After I began to believe the lies, then came the sadness and my soul's demise. I was so angry because I was so hurt, those things I never did sound so absurd! Yet hearing negative long enough I let it sink in to the point I felt hopeless with nowhere to begin.

I called on Jesus to pull me through, of course he did, he always will! I have no idea what my future holds, but I have to step up and out of the mold! The mold of what others say I am is not God's truth, it's the devil's scam!

He wants for me to be sad and hopeless, because he knows others, I can help them! He knows all too well how diamonds are made so he is hoping to keep my bright light in shade! I know God planned everything in my life, so I have to keep this in mind and fight!

Fight for my life and fight for destiny, it is so much closer than what I see. I can't look left, I can't look right, I must continue on my knees to fight! See, in my weakness Jesus is strong, he loves me even when I am wrong! He shaped my heart to love others so much, and this is why at times it hurts! Thank you, Jesus, for super human strength, please show me Lord how to begin again...

°•₀ⓜ₀•° ... °•₀ⓜ₀•° ... °•₀ⓜ₀•°

Dream Again

The letters in red O the letters in red, I can't seem to get them out of my head! I am so amazed by your love and grace, I only want to seek your face! In this life we will have pain, but no matter what your love remains! You promise me you will never leave, you love me more than I love me.

I searched high and I searched low, yet I never found a safe place to go. You began to chase me down in love, yet also through hardship and tribulation. I could hear you so clear, I knew you were near. You asked me to do things I didn't understand, I see so clearly now as you have the master plan.

Hard times still come, tears and pain, in your love Jesus I will always remain. The key to everything you want is faith, truly faith brings about unshakable strength! I have a new- found passion to live, I feel my heart learning to beat again!

For so long all I saw was rejection and shame, I truly didn't want to go on living. Every new day was stressful for me, because I had long before that stopped dreaming. I couldn't see all your promises for me, they keep sinking in the more I read. Because of you Jesus I can breathe again, you, my Lord Jesus, are my best friend!

It doesn't make life easy all of a sudden, but it does give me hope that my life goes on. I have one wish on my bucket list, that is to do as you say whenever I can. In times when I don't think I can, I will find out in my weakness is your strength! When I don't have the answers, I do have faith, and I know this verse named romans 8:28!

°•o◎o•° ... °•o◎o•° ... °•o◎o•°

A Mother's Touch

When I look at you, I see so much, so many good things but most of all love! You always do creative things, to make the greatest memories. You are great at making others smile, you always go the extra mile.

Some may look and not see what I see, I see your heart and it is so sweet! You have spent your entire life, Helping others day and night. I am so blessed to have you as my mom, what a blessing you are straight from God!

Throughout my life I didn't always treat you right, I am thankful that I finally saw the light! See, you are one of my greatest blessings, yet it took so much for me to finally see. I see strength clothed in true dignity, I see a genuinely loving woman looking back at me.

I also see a woman who has been through a lot, I know she is still standing only because of God. People in life may let you down, But God is always going to be around! He puts angels in our paths, so that even in pain and sorrow we learn to dance!

The older I get the more I see, you have always been an angel to me! I hope you know how much you are loved, I hope you know how precious you are mom. I am so glad we are best-friends, I never want these times to end. I know someday we will have to say goodbye, I know many tears we will both cry.

Yet we have this hope Jesus died for, we have mansions in Heaven and life eternal. So, no matter what we will always be together, In this world, then in Heaven forever. I love you mama, I love you so much, there is nothing quite like a mother's touch!

°•o⊙o•°   ...   °•o⊙o•°   ...   °•o⊙o•°

Wheat 100-Fold

Sometimes things in life, they hit you quick and with great surprise. When everything is going great, here comes Satan to sift you as wheat. In these moments of great pain and suffering, often they can leave you wondering.

What are you doing Lord? What is it that you want me to learn? Why do those I love have to hurt? Is everything simply to reveal our eternal worth? I don't understand, but I have come to realize sometimes I just can't.

Sometimes only you God know why, and I must see with spiritual eyes. I must see the unseen knowing you Abba are working out eternity. I fret, I cry, I pray and pray, but through it all I say Lord have your way!

In the end only you truly know, you look out for what's best through it all. I can't say that I enjoy the pain, but I can say in you I will keep my faith. Sometimes Lord I feel so weak, I wonder how I will do everything.

I feel as though I am being pulled in so many Directions I don't know what to do. Then, suddenly I look up and I realize something; This journey is not at all about me! This journey is about helping someone see your comfort, your hand, your love, your peace.

You put me in uncertain places in order to shine your love and grace. The moment I step outside of me, I begin to see a divine plan unfolding. A kind word in a hospital as I wait, wait on my loved one and their fate.

A smile or a hug, an act of love, even in time when I need someone. How quick you are to remind me you have already fulfilled all of my needs. How fast you come to my rescue if I just stop looking around and trust you!

Born again

I never thought that I would be free, free from the lies of the enemy. I am in awe of what God has done, all this is through his only begotten son. Jesus came to give life abundantly and yes o yes who he sets free is truly free!

Free from worry, free from shame and pain, When I don't feel joy and peace I just praise his holy name. Instantly he comes through for me, I am again refreshed in his glory. I don't deserve the love he gives, but I am more than thankful for it.

I am ready for what is next, I know Lord Jesus orders my steps! I have victory in his name, when I don't see I still praise him the same! There is so much power in praising his name, Jesus changed me forever, I will never be the same!

°•○◎○•° ... °•○◎○•° ... °•○◎○•°

I vow

I cry out to Jesus, I whisper his name. It seems I'm rejected for his holiness. They mock me, they say I am so perfect. 'What they don't see is I am nothing without him. Truly the devil hates holiness, so he works through others to cause me stress.

I can handle most people rejecting me, but it is really painful when it is my own family. I try so hard to love and serve, sometimes getting treatment I don't deserve. Then I remember to Jesus they did the same thing, He even died for them despised and enduring shame.

O Jesus my heart hurts please help me, O Jesus I'm weak please give me strength. I need you my Lord I truly do, My Lord and my God I cherish you. When everything is upside down, I know you are simply polishing my crown. Everything that happens is your will now, So, I will continue in your strength I vow.